Commercial Real Estate

UNDERSTANDING INVESTMENTS

EDWARD S. SMITH, JR., RECS

Dearborn™
Real Estate Education

This publication is designed to provide accurate and authoritative information in regard to the subject matter covered. It is sold with the understanding that the publisher is not engaged in rendering legal, accounting, or other professional service. If legal advice or other expert assistance is required, the services of a competent professional person should be sought.

Senior Vice President & General Manager: Roy Lipner
Publisher: Evan Butterfield
Development Editor: Anne Huston
Production Manager: Bryan Samolinski
Typesetter: Ellen Gurak
Creative Director: Lucy Jenkins

© 2002 by Dearborn Financial Publishing, Inc.®

Published by Dearborn™ Real Estate Education
a division of Dearborn Financial Publishing, Inc.®
155 North Wacker Drive
Chicago, IL 60606-1719
(312) 836-4400
http://www.dearbornRE.com

Printed in the United States of America.

02 03 04 10 09 08 07 06 05 04 03 02 01

c o n t e n t s

Chapter 4   **Property Values 23**

Chapter 5   **Introduction to Financial Analysis 35**

Chapter 6   The Value of Investments 49

Chapter 7   Forecasting Cash Flows 55

Commercial and investment real estate is an exciting and challenging area of the real estate business to work in. It gives the practitioner the opportunity to work with the presidents, CEOs and owners of businesses. Unique to this type of brokerage is the opportunity to be of service to these clients over and over again as their business requirements change or increase.

Investment properties require specific analysis and have their own "jargon," terms and formulas used in the industry. This course will teach you what you need to know and what your customers will want you to know about real estate investments. In commercial real estate, everything is referred to by initials; you will learn what PRI, NOI, CAP, CFBT, and many other abbreviations mean. Throughout the course, the actual terms used by investors will be defined and discussed. This is a "learn by doing" course, with case study problems that illustrate the learning concepts.

In the course, you will learn the principles of investment, the types and concerns of investment customers, what affects market values of properties, and how to analyze real estate investments now and in the future. When you complete this course, you will be prepared to meet the challenges and opportunities of working in investment real estate.

Mr. Edward S. Smith Jr., RECS is a licensed real estate broker, instructor, and consultant, who specializes in commercial and investment properties. He holds the Real Estate Cyberspace Specialist designation.

Mr. Smith is an Instructors Training Institute (ITI) graduate and has authored two 7.5-hour continuing education courses, which he teaches regularly: *Commercial & Investment Real Estate: Concepts and Terms* and *Commercial Real Estate: Tools of the Trade.*

As a consultant to the trade, Mr. Smith works with individual real estate offices to train their agents or to set up commercial real estate departments. He also coaches new agents to help them learn the commercial and investment real estate business.

A REALTOR®, who is active on all levels, Smith serves on the National Association of REALTORS® Commercial Alliance Committee. He is a past president of the New York State Commercial Association of REALTORS®. He serves on many committees of the New York State Association of REALTORS® including: Chairman of the Commercial Lien Law Working group; Legislative Policy; Education Management; REALTORS® Political Action Committee (REPAC) Trustee; and is a past state chairman for RPAC. Locally, he is vice president of the Long Island Commercial Network and secretary of the Commercial Industrial Brokers Society of Long Island.

■ Acknowledgements

Commercial Real Estate: Understanding Investments would not have been possible without the thoughtful feedback of commercial real estate practitioners and instructors. The author wishes to thank the following reviewers for their suggestions and contributions:

- Herbert S. Fecker Jr., CCIM, Florida Licensed Real Estate Broker, Consultant, Expert Witness, Valrico, Florida
- Syd Machat, CCIM, Director, Commercial Properties Online, Long & Foster Real Estate, Inc., Frederick, Maryland
- Dan Page, CCIM, Managing Broker, Arvida Commercial Services, Sarasota, Florida

Types of Investment Properties and Clients

overview

In commercial and investment real estate, many types of property have investment potential, and clients may be users, developers, or pure investors. This diversity provides salespersons and brokers with many combinations of opportunities to serve their clients by structuring deals for them. ■

learning objectives

After completing this lesson, you will

- know the primary classifications of commercial property,
- recognize which types of property are considered investments, and
- understand the different needs of various commercial property clients.

■ Primary Classifications of Commercial Property

There are four primary classifications of commercial property: office, retail, industrial, and apartment. Most types of commercial property fit into these general classifications. Some examples follow.

Office	*Retail*
High-Rise or Low-Rise	Free-Standing Store
Medical	Strip Center
Professional	Shopping Center and Mall
Office Condo	Outlet Center

Industrial	*Apartment*
Warehouse	Apartment Building
Distribution Center	
Factory	
Manufacturing Plant	
R&D (Research and Development)	

Because the following commercial properties are unique, they do not fall into the four general classifications.

Other Commercial Property
School
Church
Hotel
Assisted-Living, Adult, or Nursing Home

Land itself can also be commercial property. But land cannot be classified commercially until the property use is determined. Land may be developed for use strictly as commercial property, e.g., as a golf course, or for use as a residential subdivision.

■ Commercial Property as an Investment

Almost every type of commercial property can be an investment, although some are more obvious potential investments than others: an office building, a group of retail stores (strip center), or an apartment building.

When tenants, either a single tenant or multiple tenants, pay rent to a landlord, the income derived becomes a basis on which to value the property. During this course, we will examine how this value is calculated. Investors will purchase properties based upon the income produced by the tenants of that property. This concept of income potential can be applied to all types of commercial properties.

■ Commercial Investment Customers

There are three types of commercial investment customers or clients: users, developers, and pure investors.

Users

Users occupy part or all of the building or property themselves. Their business will be conducted from this location. Users are "space-driven." The size of the space and location are their primary concerns. Often they will buy a building larger than their immediate needs in order to reduce or even eliminate their rent expense.

Developers

Developers will buy land to "build-to-suit" for a specific client. Usually a lease is signed in advance, and the developer will build the client's building according to the client's specifications. Developers may also purchase an existing building to convert it to an alternative use. Sometimes they may "build on spec (speculation)," whereby they construct a building of their own design and lease it to tenants during or after the construction period. Usually, when the construction is completed and all the tenants have moved in, the developer will sell the property to a third party.

Pure Investors

Although all investors are profit driven, the "bottom line"—how much profit will be made from the investment—is the primary concern for *pure investors.* They will also consider the "upside potential" of a property: Will the value and/or the yearly profits increase for a specific reason in the future? Generally, while pure investors will not occupy space in their investments, they are very concerned with the stability of the area. Can they keep the units rented? These clients also consider an exit strategy: What will be the future value of the investment when they decide to sell it?

■ Chapter 1 Review Questions

1. Which of the following is considered commercial property?
   a. Primary residence
   b. Time share
   c. Golf course
   d. Vacation home

2. Which of these commercial properties is a potential investment?
   a. Warehouse
   b. Supermarket
   c. Office building
   d. All of the above

3. Which is true about a build-to-suit building?
   a. It is of modular construction.
   b. It is built to the tenant's specifications.
   c. It is built by a developer on "spec."
   d. It requires unusual construction materials.

4. Which phrase best describes developers?
   a. Developers are long-term investors.
   b. Developers are not investors.
   c. Developers make short-term investments.
   d. Developers buy land only.

5. What does the term "bottom line" refer to?
   a. Potential rental income
   b. Investment profit
   c. Exit strategy
   d. Employment pool

6. On what do investors base their property purchasing decisions?
   a. Income the property produces
   b. Location
   c. Size of the building
   d. Mortgage terms

Principles of Investment

overview

Commercial and investment real estate is a business based on mathematics and calculations. Common formulas are used in the industry to evaluate investment properties. The best way to learn certain concepts is through practical applications, such as the Case Study problems in this chapter.

In examining various building types, it is important to consider the different and yet similar perspectives that our clients, the "users" and the "investors," may have, or as we will see in this Chapter, how a customer can become a "User-Investor." ■

l e s s o n 1

Small Mulituse Buildings and Their Investment Potential

learning objectives

After completing this lesson, you will

■ know the characteristics of a "taxpayer" property,

■ understand the definition of and how to derive net operating income (NOI),

■ know the definition of footprint,

■ be able to forecast income potential, and

■ be able to calculate building operating expenses.

■ Defining a Taxpayer Property

A *taxpayer* property is a small multiuse building, typically a combination residential-commercial structure with retail or office space on the ground floor and apartments above. It is usually found in or near town, has a "Main Street" location, and is two or three stories high.

Historically, merchants would have their store on the ground floor and live in an apartment above. The rental income from the apartment(s) would be sufficient to pay the building's taxes. Hence, the name "taxpayer."

■ Advantages of Purchasing a Small Multiuse Building

Why would a customer buy a multiuse building today? Such a building could be attractive to either a user or investor customer. For the remainder of Lesson 1, we will discuss an investor client's considerations in purchasing a multiuse building. In Lesson 2 of this Chapter, we will examine a user customer's considerations.

The investor will look favorably toward purchasing this type of building because of its limited number of tenants, which creates a lower risk of vacancy and a consequent high level of stability. Also, this type of building will probably have a higher percentage of residential rental units, which are considered easier to rent than stores. However, the investor's primary concern will be: how much money can be made, the return on investment (ROI).

Determining rates of return on investments requires the calculation of a property's *net operating income* (NOI). In its simplest terms, net operating income (NOI) is the gross operating income (GOI) less all owner operating expenses. Operating expenses do not include income taxes or debt service (principal and interest) expenses.

> **Gross Operating Income – Owners Operating Expenses = Net Operating Income**

Commercial and investment real estate is measured and calculated in square feet. The ground floor area of a building is called the *footprint,* and it is measured in square feet. The frontage width multiplied by the depth (or length) of the ground floor of a building is the *footprint.*

case study   **Main Street Multiuse Building**

A Main Street building is two stories high. On the ground floor is a store with 25 feet of frontage and a ground floor depth of 40 feet. Upstairs are two apartments. There is a basement housing the oil heating system and storage; the basement is not rentable space.

The apartments rent for $500 each per month, and the store leases for $15 per square foot. The owner buys oil on a payment plan for $100 per month. The building's real estate taxes are $8,000 per year, and insurance costs $800 per year. The owner has no other expenses. The tenants pay their own electric and water bills.

■ Case Study Problem

What is the net operating income (NOI) of this property? Determining the net operating income is a three-part process. We have to (I) calculate the gross operating income (GOI), (II) determine the owner's operating expenses, and then (III) using these figures determine net operating income (NOI). Gross operating income

(GOI) is comprised of potential rental income (PRI), other types of income, and adjustments to income. Note that in this problem potential rental income (PRI) will be considered the total gross operating income (GOI); other income items will be discussed in subsequent Chapters.

Calculating Net Operating Income (NOI)

PART I: Determine the Potential Rental Income (PRI)

Determine the rent for all rentable space in the building, whether occupied or not, to show the total potential yearly income.

STEP 1

What is the yearly income for each apartment?

Apartment A: _____

Apartment B: _____

STEP 2

What is the yearly income for the store?

Note: Commercial rent is most often quoted as rent ($ per square foot) of the leased space. The store measures 25 feet × 40 feet = 1,000 square feet

Store Income: _____

STEP 3

What is the total potential rental income (PRI) for the building?

Solution Part I

STEP 1

Apartment A: $500 per month × 12 months = $6,000 yearly income

Apartment B: $500 per month × 12 months = $6,000 yearly income

STEP 2

Store Income: 1,000 square feet (SF) × $15 per square foot (PSF) = $15,000 yearly income

STEP 3

Apartment A:	$ 6,000
Apartment B:	6,000
Store:	15,000
Total Potential Rental Income	$ 27,000

PART II: Determine the Owner's Operating Expenses

We are concerned only with the *owner's actual expenses* on the property. What the tenants pay for has nothing to do with these calculations.

What are the owner's operating expenses (per year)?

Utilities (oil heat):	_____
Taxes:	_____
Insurance:	_____
Total Owner's Expenses:	_____

Solution Part II

Utilities (oil heat):	$ 1,200
($100 per month × 12 months)	
Taxes:	8,000
Insurance:	800
Total Owner's Operating Expenses	$ 10,000

Part III: Calculate Net Operating Income (NOI)

Remember, for this problem the potential rental income (PRI) will be considered the gross operating income (GOI).

Potential Rental Income:	$ 27,000
Owner's Operating Expenses:	−10,000
Net Operating Income (NOI) for the Building:	$ 17,000

lesson 2

Getting to the "Buy" Decision

learning objectives

After completing this lesson, you will

■   understand how it may cost less to buy than to rent a building,

■   realize the impact of debt service,

■   grasp how a User can be an Investor at the same time, and

■   have learned one of the tax advantages of ownership.

Many of our clients do not work full-time in the real estate business and may not realize the options they have. Sometimes a small business owner who has been leasing space may be unaware of the advantages of purchasing real estate.

In this lesson we will examine why a user would buy a taxpayer or larger building, that is, how this user would become a user-investor.

■ Reasons a Renter Should Purchase

A user might buy a taxpayer and become a user-investor for the following reasons:

■ Often the cost to buy is equal to or less than the cost to rent.

■ The purchase price is affordable.

■ Tax advantages of ownership.

Buying May Cost Less than Renting

In the problem just completed in Lesson 1, the store rent was calculated to be $15,000 annually ($15 PSF × 1,000 SF = $15,000 annual rent). Assuming the user buys the building, the user buyer then makes an operating profit that reduces the rent expense. From the problem, we know that the apartment rental income totals $12,000 per year, and we also know the owner's operating expenses total $10,000. By subtracting the expenses from income, a profit of $2,000 is realized.

Calculating the Buyer Profit	
Rental Income (apartments)	$12,000
Owners' Operating Expenses	−10,000
Profit:	$2,000

The user's store rent had been $15,000 a year. As the user-buyer, this rent is now reduced by the profit of $12,000 made on the building, creating an effective new store rent of $13,000.

By buying the building, the user reduced the cost to rent the store by $2,000.

Affordable Purchase Price

A small building may be relatively low in price, and the typical down payment may be only 20 percent, making a purchase affordable to the business owner.

For illustrative purposes, we will assign a sale price of $160,000 to the Lesson 1 Main Street building, and we will assume a mortgage is available for it with a 20 percent down payment, a 15-year term, and a fixed rate of 7.5 percent interest.

Financing the Main Street Building	
Building Price	$160,000
Down Payment (20%)	− 32,000
Financed Amount (Mortgage)	$128,000

It is now possible to determine the cost to "carry" the building, that is, the owner's operating expenses (which remain the same at $10,000), plus the cost of the "debt service," the annual expense of the mortgage.

Cost To Carry the Main Street Building	
Debt Service (per year)	$14,239
($128,000 mortgage for 15 years @ 7.5%interest)	
Operating Expenses	+ 10,000
Total Expenses	$24,239

The new owner still has the income from the apartments to offset these expenses. When the apartment income is subtracted from the total building's cost, the remainder is what the owner must charge himself in rent to break even on the building.

New Store Rent	
Cost To Carry the Building	$24,239
Less Income from the Apartments	− 12,000
Effective "New" Store Rent	$12,239

This is a savings of $2,761 over the original rent $15,000 due as a tenant. So the user, by becoming a buyer-owner-investor, reduces his projected rent expense by over 18 percent—from $15,000 to $12,239.

Based on an investment of $32,000 (the down payment of 20 percent of the purchase price of $160,000), our user now also investor has rent savings or *return on investment* (ROI) of $2,761 per year. In effect, in this example, he would realize a return on his investment (ROI) of 8.63 percent (.0863).

$$\$2,761 \div \$132,000 = .0863 \text{ or } 8.63\%$$

Tax Advantages of Ownership

The current Internal Revenue Service Codes allow for "depreciation," also known as "cost recovery," of commercial buildings. Depreciation is a tax deduction and, therefore, is considered a tax advantage to real estate ownership. The IRS Code has two primary rules. Buildings depreciate, but land does not. Current tax depreciation of commercial buildings extends over 39 years, with the exception of apartment buildings which depreciate over 27.5 years. (Advise clients to always discuss tax matters with their accountant or tax advisor.)

To calculate depreciation, first subtract the land value from the purchase price of the property to determine the building value. Then divide this figure by 39, for a commercial building, to find the annual amount of depreciation.

Continuing with the example, assume that the Main Street land has a value of $20 per square foot (PSF). In this case, the building is a "postage stamp," meaning the land is the same size as the footprint of the building. We know from the problem that the footprint of the building is 1,000 square feet (SF); therefore, 1,000 SF × $20 (PSF) = $20,000 land value.

Tax Advantage of Ownership	
Purchase Price	$160,000
Less Land Value	− 20,000
Depreciable Building Value	$140,000

The building value divided by 39 years equals the annual tax depreciation.

$140,000 ÷ 39 = $3,590 Tax Advantage

By buying the building, the user-investor saves $2,761 in rent and has a tax advantage of $3,590. Real estate agents should discuss the advantages of purchasing with their clients.

■ Chapter 2 Review Questions

1. A small two-story multiuse building with a store below and two apartments above has historically been referred to as a
   a. strip center.
   b. good investment.
   c. R&D property.
   d. taxpayer.

2. The square footage of the ground floor of a building is known as the
   a. footprint.
   b. area.
   c. dimensions.
   d. usable area.

3. The potential rental income less all owner operating expenses is the
   a. bottom line.
   b. return on investment.
   c. net operating income.
   d. profit percentage.

4. Over how many years is the current IRS depreciation of commercial buildings?
   a. 31
   b. 39
   c. 7
   d. 10

5. If a person buys a commercial parcel of land, how much of the property is tax depreciable?
   a. 100%
   b. 80%
   c. 20%
   d. 0%

6. Why would a customer buy a building instead of renting?
   a. The cost to buy may be less than the cost to rent.
   b. It may be affordable and a good investment.
   c. There are tax advantages of ownership.
   d. All of the above

7. What is NOT considered a typical operating expense of a building?
   a. Real estate taxes
   b. Debt service
   c. Insurance
   d. Heating fuel

8. What is included in potential rental income?
   a. All possible rent for the building
   b. Only rent from occupied spaces
   c. Rent after adjustment for vacancy
   d. Rent actually collected

9. What is annual debt service?
   a. The total expenses for a property
   b. The total yearly mortgage expense
   c. The monthly expense payments
   d. A management company

10. Who may be among the buyers of commercial properties?
    a. Users
    b. Investors
    c. User-investors
    d. All of the above

Contingency Adjustments and Expenses

overview

In Chapter 2 we saw how to determine the first component of property valuation, the net operating income (NOI). In this Chapter, we will expand the considerations used in calculating net operating income (NOI) to include certain contingencies. Lesson 1 will examine the effects of "Vacancy and Credit Loss" adjustments on income, and Lesson 2 will examine "Repair and Maintenance" expenses. A "Neighborhood Strip Center" will serve as a Case Study to further illustrate these concepts. ■

lesson 1 — Vacancy Allowances and Credit Losses

learning objectives

After completing this lesson, you will

■ know the definitions of vacancy and credit loss expenses,

■ be able to estimate vacancy factors,

■ see the effect of vacancy on investments, and

■ recognize the features of a neighborhood strip center.

■ The Concept of Vacancy

Vacancy is defined as a portion of, or an entire space, without tenancy, measured for a period of time. From a investor's point of view, potential vacancy is measured as an contingent expense adjustment to the potential rental income (PRI), *usually in percentage terms.* For example:

> **Potential Rental Income – Vacancy Contingency = Effective Rental Income**

$$\$200,000 - \$20,000 \text{ (i.e., 10\%)} = \$180,000$$

Determining the percentage of vacancy is a "reality" issue. What is the probability that one or more of the rental units will be vacant during the year and for how long will it or they be vacant?

A factor in making this determination is dictated by the size of the building and the number of tenants. A big building with a large number of tenants tends to reduce the percentage of vacancy.

The main question then becomes: If the space becomes vacant, how long will it take to rent it? Vacancy expense is a function of time.

■ Credit Losses

The complete term for the vacancy category is "vacancy and credit losses." Remember, in financial analysis, vacancy and credit losses are deducted "off the top," directly from potential rental income (PRI) before any expenses.

Credit losses include rent lost due to nonpayment by a tenant. The tenant may move out overnight or declare bankruptcy. Credit losses are considered part of the vacancy income adjustment.

■ Neighborhood Strip Center

A *Neighborhood Strip Center* is any shopping area, generally with common parking, comprised of a row of stores. Usually it does not contain major department stores or grocery chain stores. Typically, it is a single building divided into five to ten stores. Which type of customer would be most likely to buy a neighborhood strip center?

Considerations of a User Customer

In the last chapter, we noted three advantages for a user to buy rather than lease space. Two of those reasons would apply to a neighborhood strip center if our customer was going to conduct his or her business from one of the stores in that center.

1. The cost to buy may be equal to or less than the cost to rent. One would expect that the purchase would reduce the cost, rent, for his or her store.
2. Tax advantages of ownership. Cost recovery through tax deductions available for depreciation would certainly be advantageous.

However, the affordable purchase price may no longer be true. Typically, a neighborhood strip center is a larger, more expensive property to purchase than a taxpayer. The acquisition price for the center could be out of reach for a small business owner.

Considerations of an Investor Client

An investor would most likely purchase a neighborhood strip center after evaluating the following points:

■ Quality of the tenants (relatively few tenants could be good or bad)
■ Turnover (vacancy) concerns (competition - what's going on in the area)
■ Rate of return on the investment (profit potential)

Investors are concerned with the bottom line, how much profit can they make, and the stability of the investment, can they keep it rented. Profit is measured as the cash flow a property produces, what is left after all the expenses have been paid. We will discuss cash flow in more detail in Chapter 6.

case study   Neighborhood Strip Center

The neighborhood strip center in this Case Study consists of 12,000 square feet of land improved by a 5,000 square-foot building and a paved parking lot. The building is divided into five stores; each store is 1,000-square feet. There is no basement; each store has their own gas heating, ventilating and air-conditioning system (HVAC) on the roof. Tenants have separate meters and pay for their own gas and electric. The stores rent for $15 per square foot (PSF).

The owner's property taxes are $20,000 a year. The owner has only one other itemized operating expense, in this case, $2,500 a year for insurance.

Current *rent roll* includes:

- Video store (occupies two storefronts)
- Pizza parlor
- Dry cleaner
- Vacant store

■ Case Study Problem

Determine the net operating income (NOI) of this property.

To do this analysis, we will break the problem down into several steps, as enumerated below. Solutions to these steps are found on page 18. The first step is to determine the Potential Rental Income (PRI).

STEP 1: Calculate Potential Rental Income (PRI)

Potential rental income (PRI) will include projected income from any vacant units (stores). It is reasonable to assume, in this problem, that the projected rent from the vacant store will be the same as the rent that the others stores pay. The video store occupies two storefronts of 1,000 SF each for a total leased space of 2,000 SF.

Calculating Potential Rental Income (PRI)			
	Size (SF)	Rent ($ PSF)	Annual Rent
Video store	_____	× _____	_____
Pizza parlor	_____	× _____	_____
Dry cleaner	_____	× _____	_____
Vacant store	_____	× _____	_____
Total Potential Rental Income			_____

Step 2: Adjusting for Vacancy

After establishing the potential rental income (PRI) of the property, it is appropriate to make a contingency adjustment for vacancy. Vacancy is usually calculated as a percentage of the potential rental income (PRI).

To determine the vacancy percentage requires a "reality examination" of the property and the surrounding area. How many other stores are available for rent in comparable buildings in the local area?

For illustrative purposes in this example of five stores, we will assume one store will be unoccupied for six months a year. Now we can convert this information to a vacancy rate percentage.

Determining Vacancy Percentage

Neighborhood Strip Center store unoccupied for six months a year.

PART 1

Calculate the projected *monthly* rent for that store

- Size of the store = 1,000 SF
- Projected Annual Rent @ $15 PSF
- 1,000 SF × $15 PSF = $15,000 Annual Rent
- $15,000 ÷ 12 months = $1,250 rent per month

PART 2

Calculate the lost income potential

- Monthly rent × projected vacancy period = lost income potential
- $1,250 (monthly rent) × 6 months (projected unoccupied time) = $7,500
- This is also the vacancy contingency amount ($).

Vacancy Percentage Rate is the vacancy contingency amount ($) divided by the total Potential Rental Income.

$$\frac{\text{Vacancy Contingency Amount}}{\text{Potential Rental Income}} = \frac{\$7,500}{\$75,000} = .10$$

Vacancy Percentage Rate   10%

Here is another example. If there were ten stores in the strip center instead of five stores, with all else being equal (each store 1,000 SF, rent @ $15 PSF), one store vacant, the rate would be calculated as follows. The total projected rental income (PRI) for 10 stores would be:

1,000 SF × $15 PSF = $15,000 (potential income per store) × 10 Stores = $150,000 PRI

One store vacant ($1,250 monthly rent × 6 months) =
$7,500 Vacancy Contingency Amount

Again, the vacancy contingency amount divided by the potential rental income (PRI) equals the vacancy percentage rate. In this example:

$7,500 (Vacancy Contingency Amount) ÷ $150,000 (PRI) = .05
5% Vacancy Rate

Remember, the vacancy expense rate requires a "reality check" that may include examining vacancies in similar buildings in the area. What is the vacancy rate in the general market area of the property?

We have determined the potential rental income (PRI) for the five-store neighborhood strip center to be $75,000. The vacancy percentage has been estimated as 10 percent. This is an income adjustment made by subtracting the calculated vacancy dollar amount from the potential rental income (PRI). The result is the effective rental income (ERI), which in this case will be the same as the gross operating income. (This distinction is further defined in Chapter 5.)

Gross Operating Income (GOI)

Potential Rental Income (PRI)	$75,000
Vacancy Adjustment of 10%	– _____
Gross Operating Income (GOI)	_____

STEP 3: Calculating the Total Operating Expenses

This step determines the annual expenses paid by the owner.

Operating Expenses

Real Estate Taxes	$_____
Insurance	$_____
Total Operating Expenses	$_____

STEP 4: Calculating Net Operating Income (NOI)

The case study has asked us to determine the net operating income (NOI).

Net Operating Income (NOI)

Gross Operating Income (GOI)	$_____
Operating Expenses	– $_____
Net Operating Income (NOI)	$_____

Solution Determining Net Operating Income (NOI)

STEP 1

Video store	2,000 SF	×	$15 PSF	$30,000
Pizza parlor	1,000 SF	×	$15 PSF	15,000
Dry cleaner	1,000 SF	×	$15 PSF	15,000
Vacant store	1,000 SF	×	$15 PSF	+15,000
Total Potential Rental Income (PRI)				$75,000

STEP 2

Potential Rental Income (PRI)	$75,000
Vacancy Adjustment (10%)	− 7,500
Gross Operating Income (GOI)	$67,500

STEP 3

Property taxes	$20,000
Insurance	+ 2,500
Total Operating Expenses	$22,500

STEP 4

Gross Operating Income (GOI)	$67,500
Operating Expenses	− 22,500
Net Operating Income (NOI)	$45,000

les**2**on

Repairs and Maintenance

learning objectives

After completing this lesson, you will

■ know the difference between contingency and regular expenses,

■ understand the concept of "Repair and Maintenance" expense,

■ be able to estimate percentages of contingency expenses, and

■ know the effect of repairs and maintenance on investments.

■ Contingency Expenses

"Repair and Maintenance" is a contingency expense item that often, but not always, takes the form of a percentage adjustment. It is similar to the vacancy income adjustment in that it too requires a "reality examination."

The repair and maintenance contingency is one of the categories of operating expenses. Examples of other operating expenses are service contracts for *routine maintenance*, i.e., landscaping, snow removal, cleaning and security; real estate taxes; property insurance; legal fees; accounting; employees; management; supplies, etc. It is important to make a distinction under the operating expenses between (1) normal, regular, maintenance expenses and (2) contingency repair and maintenance expenses. Contingency expenses are best thought of as irregular, unexpected, or emergency events.

Continuing to examine the Case Study of the Neighborhood Strip Center from Lesson 1 in this Chapter, there are two parts of the property that could require unexpected repair and maintenance, the building itself or the parking lot.

For example, in the case of the parking lot, *normal regular expenses* would include landscaping, snow removal, lighting, or cleanup. In many cases, normal regular expenses are contracted out. A contingency maintenance expense item might include sealing the blacktop lot when needed or restriping the parking space lines.

In the Case Study problem, the landlord provides heating, ventilating, and air-conditioning (HVAC) systems for each tenant. The tenants pay for gas and electric, but it is up to the owner to keep each HVAC unit in good working order. If the unit breaks down, the landlord must pay for its repair, or replace the unit. This would be a contingency repair expense.

The landlord may employ a person to do a variety of tasks, and "payroll" and related expenses would be considered normal regular expenses.

What about the building's roof? How old is it? Is it under guarantee? How long does a roof last? What does it cost to replace a roof? Anticipating a roof repair or replacement would be an item considered and included as a repair and maintenance contingency expense.

■ Calculating Repair and Maintenance Contingency Expenses

Generally, in property analysis, Repair and Maintenance is a percentage of the potential rental income (PRI) or the gross operating income (GOI). Because investors differ on which figures they use as a basis for these calculations, you must always define how the expense figure was determined.

Note, however, in some cases a dollar figure is used instead of a percentage. For example, in a case where it is known that a heating system is old and is expected to be replaced within three years, the anticipated cost may be averaged out and a fixed dollar figure used.

When a percentage is used to calculate repair and maintenance expense, what percentage rate should that be?

This is another "reality" issue—to get to repair and maintenance expense, consider the building and other things that could require repair or maintenance (i.e., parking lot) and, most importantly, the lease obligations.

The three primary guidelines are as follows:

1. Age and condition of the building
2. Condition and other improvements to the property
3. The landlord's responsibilities under the lease

A lease defines the duties of the landlord and the tenant. It tells us who is responsible for what. In a Triple Net lease, (NNN) for example, the tenant is generally responsible for all repairs and maintenance. In such a case, the landlord's repair and maintenance contingency expense *percentage* could be very low or none.

As a general rule of thumb, repair and maintenance is usually calculated at 5 percent to 10 percent of the potential rental income (PRI) and is included under the operating expenses of the property. However, remember that some investors take a percentage of the gross operating income (GOI) and some use a specific dollar amount. Always clarify which is being used. Let's see how this adjustment changes the net operating income (NOI) in the neighborhood strip center Case Study from Lesson 1.

■ Repair and Maintenance Problem

Following you will find a recap of the first problem involving the neighborhood strip center from Lesson 1. Now, *calculate the repair and maintenance expense*, the *total operating expenses,* and *the new net operating income (NOI)* in the next exercise. For this example, we will assume the building is only five years old and in very good condition; use 5% of the potential rental income (PRI) to calculate the repair and maintenance expense. Check your answers against the solution on page 21.

Neighborhood Strip Center - Rent Roll Recap

Video store	$30,000
Pizza parlor	15,000
Dry cleaner	15,000
Vacant (projected)	+15,000
Projected Rental Income (PRI)	$75,000
[Vacancy and Credit Losses (10%)]	−7,500
Gross Operating Income (GOI)	$67,500

Neighborhood Strip Center Problem

Operating Expenses	
Real Estate Taxes	$20,000
Insurance	2,500
Repair & Maintenance (__%)	_____
Total Operating Expenses	_____
Net Operating Income	_____

Solution—New Net Operating Income (NOI) with Repair and Maintenance Contigency Expenses

Operating Expenses	
Real Estate Taxes	$20,000
Insurance	2,500
Repair & Maintenance (5%)	+3,750
Total Operating Expenses	$26,250

Repair & Maintenance = 5% of the Potential Rental Income (PRI)

$$.05 \times \$75,000 = \$3,750$$

Gross Operating Income – Total Operating Expenses = Net Operating Income (NOI)

$$\$67,500 - \$26,250 = \$41,250$$

Net Operating Income	$41,250

With a "reality" analysis of the neighborhood strip center, including vacancy and repair and maintenance contingency expenses, we have determined it to have a net operating income (NOI) of $41,250. We will see later in Chapter 4 how the NOI relates to property values.

■ Chapter 3 Review Questions

1. What type of store is typically not found in a Neighborhood Strip Center?
   a. Video store
   b. Pizza parlor
   c. Supermarket
   d. Dry cleaners

2. What is potential vacancy considered by an investor?
   a. Loss factor
   b. Income adjustment
   c. Reduced return on investment
   d. Credit loss

3. Vacancy is a portion or entire space without tenancy
   a. based on the size of the building.
   b. converted to a dollar expense.
   c. based on the number of tenants.
   d. for a period of time.

4. Potential rental income less adjustments for vacancy and credit losses results in the
   a. net operating income.
   b. gross operating expenses.
   c. vacancy contingency.
   d. gross operating income.

5. What would result in "credit losses?"
   a. Tenant vacates the space without notice.
   b. Tenant declares bankruptcy.
   c. Tenant is evicted for not paying rent.
   d. All of the above

6. The vacancy percentage is
   a. a constant.
   b. determined "case by case."
   c. a formula.
   d. always 10%.

7. What is an example of an operating expense?
   a. Landscape contract
   b. Repair and maintenance
   c. Accounting fees
   d. All of the above

8. Which would be considered an irregular, unexpected, or emergency expense?
   a. Advertising
   b. Security
   c. Roof repair
   d. Snow removal

9. By definition, which would be a contingent repair and maintenance expense?
   a. Landscaping
   b. Cleaning
   c. A hired maintenance man
   d. None of the above

10. Repair and maintenance can be calculated as a percentage of
    a. gross operating income.
    b. total operating expenses.
    c. building size.
    d. property size.

Property Values

overview

This chapter examines the market value of properties—what they are today and what they could be tomorrow. It also explores the ramifications of changing a property's use.

The investor looks at property from a "potential profit" point of view and uses formulas to analyze value. In Chapter 2 and Chapter 3, you were introduced to the concept of net operating income (NOI); in this chapter you will see how this leads to a capitalization rate (CAP rate), a basis used to determine market value. ■

lesson 1

Understanding Market Value

learning objectives

After completing this lesson, you will

■ be able to define market value,

■ understand the concept of highest and best use,

■ know the definition of floor area ratio (FAR),

■ understand the cost of zoning, and

■ be able to compare the value of a land lease to a sale.

■ Market Value

The Appraisal Foundation publishes this basic definition of *market value:*

The most probable price a property would bring in a competitive and open market under all conditions requisite to a fair sale. The buyer and seller each acting prudently and knowledgeably, and assuming the price is not affected by undue stimulus.

"Fair" market value can more simply be looked at as both the buyer and seller feeling that they each got a "good deal."

Within this concept one must also ask, "why will one investor pay more money for a property than another investor." What does timing have to do with a sale?

Market value is what one person is willing to pay for a certain property *at a particular point in time*. As time changes, his or her need or desire for the property may change, too: It may be worth more or less to the potential buyer. Sellers are affected in the same way. A homeowner trying to move in the summer—to minimize the effect of the move on his child's school year—may accept a lower offer in July than in April or May.

Because some businesses are seasonal, being asked to move in the height of a busy selling season would certainly require additional compensation. What is important to the individual sellers dictates their motivation and the price.

■ Market Conditions Affecting Price

When a salesperson sells a house, the following market conditions can affect the price:

- *Supply and Demand*—Availability of this *type of house* at this particular time. Considerations include:
  - Size of home and property
  - Price and current financing opportunities
    - As supply dwindles and demand increases, prices go up.
- *Location, location, location*—Often considered the major attribute of a home. Considerations include:
  - Quality of the school district
  - Access to transportation
    - For example, some people who live in suburbs but work in the city may seek a location where they can walk to a railroad station.
    - Some folks require easy access to public transportation to take them to shopping or work.
  - To some buyers the most important thing is a quiet street in a quiet area; others prefer "busy" areas.

Will a buyer pay more money for the same basic house in a different area? Absolutely!

■ Other Factors Affecting Price

Besides the buyer's desire for the house, the following factors can affect the price:

- *Available Financing*—Will the buyer be able to afford his or her dream house? The amount of financing available dictates the required down payment. The mortgagee, usually a bank, will be looking at the *appraised value* and *comparable sales* (comps) in the area and then will determine its own *maximum* value for the house. In times of escalating prices, often there will not be sufficient data (comps) to justify the requested mortgage amount, and the buyer may have to increase the down payment to proceed with the purchase. Or the owner may have to reduce his or her asking price to make the house finance-able in such a market.

■ *Insurance Value*—What would it cost to build or rebuild the house today? Today's construction costs are of concern to the mortgagor and the insurer. Is the market value the same as the construction cost? It could be higher or lower.

■ Understanding Commercial Market Value

Would a commercial buyer pay more money for the same building in a more desir-able location? Some buyers will consider other things as assets to a commercial building's value and pay more for that property. Points of influence may be the following:

■ *For a Retailer*
  ■ Better location
  ■ More traffic for the store—busier street
  ■ New market—an area that is building up, increasing in population
  ■ Less competition
■ *For an Industrialist*
  ■ More efficient building—perfect design for the business
  ■ Larger or "cheaper" workforce
  ■ Transportation advantages
    ■ Closer to main highways—less trucking expense
    ■ Rail siding availability
■ *For a Pure Investor*
  ■ Better location—could drive the rents higher but could also increase the acquisition price
  ■ More population density—less chance of vacancy
  ■ Upside potential—future value of the property

Other commercial customers will have a somewhat flexible attitude about the location of the property. They will base a building's value on construction costs, as insurance companies do. A warehouse user may evaluate a building by asking the question: What would it cost to build the same building on another site? How does the price per square foot as a resale compare with the cost of new construc-tion? This concept tends to stabilize the industrial markets, property values somewhat.

■ Understanding Investment Market Value

Market values of investment properties, traditionally office buildings and those of the apartment or habitational class, are dictated by the financial performances of those properties. Individual commercial and investment buyers will consider dif-ferent "points" in deciding their market value of a property and make offers accordingly. However, many of the same concerns as in residential real estate can effect commercial transactions: The ability to finance, appraised value, and comparable sales.

■ Highest and Best Use

The best use of a property will create the highest financial return on investment. To determine "highest and best use," we must look at the site from both a "vacant land" and "improved property" (with building[s] on it) perspective. This means giving consideration to changing the use, design, or size of an existing building, or removing any existing structure(s) in order to approach the property as raw land.

Investors must evaluate the physical qualities of the property, topography, access (curb cuts), required setbacks, and current zoning permits. The feasibility of a change in zoning or use and how long it will take must be investigated.

While pursuing a zoning change or variance, the property may be off the market in a subject-to-sale condition for a considerable period of time. This raises the question of who will "carry" the property during that time? Who pays the real estate taxes, existing mortgage, expenses, etc., while the zoning change is being pursued?

Besides the legal and professional costs of zoning changes or variances, three other considerable direct costs may be involved in changing the use of a property:

1. Cost to demolish existing structure(s).
2. The construction cost of a new building versus the cost of renovation or expansion of an existing building.
3. Downtime expense—a period of no rental income from the property. This generally occurs during the construction or renovation period, after the prior tenant has moved out until the new tenant moves in and commences rent payments.

Such expenses must be weighed when evaluating the financial impact of a contemplated change of use.

How much more income will result from the new use? Does the "deal" make economic sense?

Before looking at highest and best use case problems, it is important to understand two more terms used in commercial applications: triple net lease (NNN) and floor area ratio (FAR).

■ Triple Net Lease (NNN)

In the triple net lease (NNN), the tenant generally pays *all* expenses for the leased space, including real estate taxes, utilities, repairs, insurance, etc.

■ Floor Area Ratio (FAR)

Floor area ratio (FAR), also known as the land coverage ratio, is the ratio of the bulk area of a building to the land on which it is situated. It is calculated by dividing the total square footage of the building by the total square footage of the land.

Usually the floor area ratio is expressed in zoning codes in statements such as: A building's size may not exceed a FAR of 25 percent, or a FAR of 40 percent. The percentage allowed will vary based on the type of building and the exact location.

For example, if a building is three stories high and each floor is 1,000 SF, the total square footage of the building would be 3,000. If the building was situated on a 10,000 SF parcel of land, the FAR would be 30 percent.

Total Building SF ÷ Total Land SF = Floor Area Ratio

3,000 SF (building) ÷ 10,000 SF (land) = .30 or 30% FAR

■ Highest and Best Use Problem A

Presently a 20,000 SF corner parcel of land is improved by a 3,000 SF building used as a gas station. The owner is paid $20 PSF, NNN (per square foot, triple net lease), and the lease expires in six months. A convenience store wants to lease the corner, but it needs 4,000 SF; they offer to pay the same $20 PSF, NNN.

In checking the zoning, the owner finds that the floor area ratio (FAR) is 25 percent and that use as a convenience store will require a "variance" from the local zoning board. The owner then calls his attorney who tells him the use should be approved but that the process takes 6 months, and his fee will be $5,000. Next, the owner gets construction estimates and finds that expanding the building from 3,000 SF to 4,000 SF will cost $40 PSF and will take three months to complete.

Evaluate the convenience store's proposal and determine if this is a "good deal" for the owner.

Problem A involves determining if the project is feasible from a zoning point of view and if the financial expense of conversion is worth the projected financial gain. We will begin with the considerations involved and then show solutions to each step.

Considerations in Evaluating the Conveniece Store Proposal

STEP 1

Evaluate Zoning Issues

The owner's attorney indicated that he believed a variance to allow a change of use from a gas station to a convenience store would be granted. The other consideration is if the proposed increase in the size of the building would be permitted under the current zoning requirements for floor area ratio (FAR). *Calculate the floor area ratio (FAR) for the proposed building.*

STEP 2

Compare current net operating income (NOI) to proposed net operating income (NOI)

To review, the net operating income (NOI) is calculated by subtracting the total operating expenses (TOE) from the gross operating income (GOI). In the case of an absolute triple net lease (NNN) there will be no operating expenses. *Calculate the net operating income (NOI) of the current tenant and the NOI of the proposed tenants lease.*

STEP 3

Estimate Conversion Costs

Consideration must be made for *all* expenses to convert the use of the property including legal expenses for zoning approvals, construction costs, and downtime (periods of time without rental income). *Calculate the total conversion costs.*

Solution Highest and Best Use Problem A

STEP 1

Floor area ratio (FAR)—The ratio of the bulk area of a building to the land on which it is situated—is calculated by dividing the total square footage of the building by the total square footage of the land.

4,000 SF (proposed building) ÷ 20,000 SF (size of land) = .20 or 20% FAR

Because the ratio, 20%, is below the zoning limit of 25% in this problem, the proposed building expansion would be permitted.

STEP 2

Remember, gross operating income (GOI) minus total operating expenses (TOE) equals net operating income (NOI).

Existing Tenant:

    Rent $20 PSF × 3,000 SF = $60,000 annual rent

    Total Income $60,000 – Total Expenses $0 (due to NNN lease) = $60,000 NOI

Proposed Tenant:

    Rent $20 PSF × 4,000 SF = $80,000 annual rent

    Total Income $80,000 – Total Expenses $0 (due to NNN lease) = $80,000 NOI

The comparison of income in step 2 seems to show that the proposal makes good financial sense, but it is also necessary to consider the conversion costs.

> **Solution** *Highest and Best Use Problem A (continued)*
>
> **STEP 3:**
> Conversion Costs
>
> Legal cost of variance = $5,000
>
> There is no downtime in this category; the problem tells us the time to get a variance will be six months and the time remaining on the current tenant's lease is six months. The variance can be obtained before the lease expires. No loss of rent will occur during the change of zoning.
>
> Construction cost = $40,000
>
> The owner must expand the existing building from 3,000 SF to 4,000 SF.
> The problem states that construction costs are $40 per square foot. Added space 1,000 SF × $40 PSF = $40,000.
>
> Downtime = $15,000
>
> There is no rental income during the three-month construction period. The lost rental income is calculated on what the owner is currently receiving. Current annual rent of $60,000 divided by 12 months = $5,000 current monthly rent. Construction time of 3 months × $5,000 monthly rent = $15,000 "downtime" expense.
>
> | | |
> |---|---|
> | Variance legal cost | $ 5,000 |
> | Construction cost | 40,000 |
> | Downtime lost rent | +15,000 |
> | Total Conversion Cost | $ 60,000 |

Summary

Keeping it simple, as seen in Figure 4.2, this is a "good deal" for most owners for the following reasons:

- The new proposed tenant will increase the owner's net operating income (NOI) $20,000 per year.
- On a cash basis, the owner could recover his conversion costs of $60,000 in 3 years.
- Thereafter, the owner could clear an additional $20,000 per year in rent from the new tenant.

■ Highest and Best Use Problem B

Our client owns a 20,000 square foot (SF) site improved with a 3,000 square foot (SF) building used as a gas station. The lease has expired, but the landlord and tenant have a mutual understanding that the tenant may stay on a month-to-month basis. The owner asked her real estate broker to sell the property for $600,000.

The current tenant pays $25 per square foot (PSF) NET to the owner. The owner's only expense is taxes of $15,000 per year. The tenant pays all other expenses.

The broker offers the property to one of his fast food customers (recognizing a zoning change would be required), and they make the following proposal:

- They wish to "land lease" the property for a term of 20 years at $60,000 per year triple net lease, with 8% rent increases every five years.
- The lease will be "subject to" their obtaining zoning approval for a 5,000 square foot restaurant building on the site.
- They will pay for all costs to obtain the zoning approvals, to demolish the current building, and to construct the new building.

What is the "best deal" for the owner?

This problem presents several issues to explore. The proposal is for a land lease, but the sales agent has been directed to sell the property. In commercial real estate, it is not uncommon for an owner to change from desiring to sell the property to entertaining a lease (or visa-versa); it is simply based on a good business decision. With this in mind, we will evaluate this proposal.

Evaluating the Fast Food Tenant's Proposal

STEP 1

Compare net operating income

Calculate the net operating income for the current tenant and for the proposed tenant.

Solution

Gross Operating Income – Total Operating Expenses = Net Operating Income

Current Tenant:

Gross Operating Income ($25 PSF × 3,000 SF)	$75,000
Total Operating Expense (Taxes)	– 15,000
Net Operating Income	$60,000

Proposed Tenant:

Gross Operating Income (Land Lease)	$60,000
– Total Operating Expenses (NNN Lease)	– 0
Net Operating Income (NOI)	$60,000

It appears that both NOIs are the same, but is this really the case? Under the current NET lease, the owner collects more rent but pays the tax expenses himself. The proposed triple net lease (NNN), (whereby the tenant pays all expenses, yields the owner the same money he is receiving currently at this time. But what happens if the taxes increase in the future?

Evaluating the Fast Food Tenant's Proposal (continued)

If the taxes increased to $20,000 under the current lease the owner's net opertating income would decrease.

Gross Operating Income	$75,000
Total Operating Expenses	– 20,000
Net Operating Income	$55,000

However, under the proposed triple net lease, the new tenant would be paying the taxes and there would be no change to the owner's income.

Gross Operating Income	$60,000
Total Operating Expenses	– 0
Net Operating Income	$60,000

Tax increases under the proposed lease are borne by the tenant, not the owner. Under a triple net lease, the owners net operating income would not be affected if the expenses (which are paid by the tenant) go up.

It is important to note the benefit to an owner of a triple net lease with regard to possible future increases in real estate taxes.

STEP 2

Evaluate Other Conditions of the Offer

- Current lease has no rent increases; the proposed lease has defined rent increases in the future, 8% every five years.

- The proposal has no conversion expenses; the new tenants do all the demolition and construction at their expense.

- There is no downtime because this is a land lease that starts when the new tenants get their approvals. The existing tenant, who is now renting month to month, could stay until the new lease commences.

- Because this is a land lease, there will be no downtime for construction. Once the approvals are obtained, rent will be paid to the owner. The owner does not have to wait for a building to be constructed to collect rent. (In other cases, the subject-to conditions of an offer may state: Rent to commence upon occupancy or upon receiving the certificate of occupancy (CO) for the new building, in which case there would be downtime.

■ Another Benefit of Land Leases

Another benefit is associated with land leases. At the end of a land lease any buildings on the site, even if erected by the tenants at their cost, belong to the property owner.

In this problem, at the end of the 20-year-lease term, the owner will have a 5,000 square foot building on his property, presumably worth more than the current 3,000 square foot structure originally on the site.

■ What is the Best Deal for the Owner?

What is the best "deal" for our client: To sell the property for $600,000 or to land lease for $60,000 per year triple net lease (NNN)? If the client does not need to sell the property, which could subject her to capital gains taxes and significantly reduce her after-tax yield, the land lease could be a good deal for her.

In this case, the lease offers Triple Net protection, eliminating the concern that the cost of expenses may increase, e.g., real estate taxes go up. The proposal gives the owner upside potential because of defined rent escalations, and it increases the future value of the property because of the larger building on it.

Hint: As real estate practitioners, if the owner needs to sell the property now, you may be able to sell the property to an investor developer as one transaction and then bring this proposal to the new owner as a second transaction.

Capitalization Rate (CAP rate)

learning objectives

After completing this lesson, you will

■ know the formula for calculating the capitalization rate (CAP rate), and

■ know how to use the capitalization rate (CAP rate) formula to determine market value.

The capitalization rate (CAP rate) can be looked at as a desired "profit percentage" for an investor. It is based on the premise that a correlation exists between the income a property produces and its value. By using a capitalization rate (CAP rate), a market value can be determined. This concept is also referred to as the "Income Approach" to determining value.

■ CAP Rate Formula to Solve for Market Value

Net Operating Income (NOI) divided by the Capitalization Rate (CAP rate) equals Market Value.

$$\text{NOI} \div \text{CAP rate} = \text{Market Value}$$

Here is an example.

A property has a NOI of $50,000. The investor's desired profit percentage—or capitalization rate (CAP rate) is 10 percent. What is the market value of the property?

$$\$50,000 \text{ NOI} \div .10 \ (10\%) \text{ CAP rate} = \$500,000 \text{ Market Value}$$

What are we demonstrating? An investor will pay $500,000 for a building. The net operating income (NOI) of the building is $50,000; this gives the investor a 10 percent return on the investment. We are not considering financing at this time.

■ Formula to Solve for the CAP Rate

Net Operating Income divided by the Market Value equals the Capitalization Rate (CAP rate)

NOI ÷ Market Value = CAP rate

Here is an example. A property has a NOI of $60,000. A buyer offers to purchase it for $500,000. What is the capitalization rate (CAP rate)?

$60,000 (NOI) ÷ $500,000 (Market Value) = .12 or 12% CAP rate

■ Practice CAP Rate Problems

CAP Rate Problem A

A property is priced at $750,000 and has a net operating income (NOI) of $67,000. What is the capitalization rate (CAP rate) being offered? Check your answer against the one found below.

CAP Rate Problem B

An investor wants to sell her building. She advises you that she has a net operating income (NOI) of $48,000 and will offer the property at an 11% capitalization rate (CAP rate). At what price do you market the building? See below.

Solution – CAP Rate Problem A

The formula for solving for the capitalization rate (CAP rate) is as follows:

NOI ÷ Market Value = CAP rate $67,000 ÷ $750.000 = .0893 or 9%

The CAP rate (rounded off) is 9%.

Solution – CAP Rate Problem B

NOI ÷ CAP rate = Market Value $48,000 ÷ .11 = $436,363

The Market Value may be rounded off to $436,000.

■ Other Valuation Methods

To conclude this section on market value, you should be aware of another valuation method called the discounted cash flow model. The discounted cash flow method looks at the property for the entire period it is expected to be held. It forecasts the projected net operating income (NOI) for each year and estimates the sale price of the property at the end of the holding period. Current market discount rates are factored, and present value is calculated. This data will also be used to calculate *internal rate of return (IRR)*, which is a percentage reflecting the return on the investment for the entire holding period.

This may sound complicated: It is, and it is appropriately taught in more advanced commercial and investment courses. The discounted cash flow method is only mentioned here so you know of its existence and some of the terminology involved.

■ Chapter 4 Review Questions

1. What is a common concern of BOTH residential and commercial real estate buyers?
   a. Appraised value
   b. School districts
   c. Vacancy
   d. All of the above

2. Given an NOI of $87,000 and a price of $800,000, what return is being offered to an investor?
   a. 9.19%
   b. 6.96%
   c. 10.88%
   d. 12.00%

3. The timing of a sale of any real estate dictates
   a. price.
   b. motivation.
   c. negotiations.
   d. all of the above.

4. When a tenant pays ALL the expenses for their leased space, it is called a
   a. gross lease.
   b. net lease.
   c. triple net lease.
   d. percentage lease.

5. The ratio of the bulk area of a building to the land on which it is situated is known the
   a. footprint.
   b. floor area ratio.
   c. site ratio.
   d. percentage of use.

6. The best use of the property to create the highest financial return is referred to as
   a. return on investment.
   b. capitalization rate.
   c. highest and best use.
   d. triple net income.

7. At the end of a land lease, if the tenant constructed a building on the site, what happens to the building?
   a. The tenant is compensated for the cost of construction.
   b. The building is removed.
   c. The building becomes the property of the land owner.
   d. None of the above

8. What is considered a "profit percentage" for an investor?
   a. Net operating income
   b. Gross operating income
   c. Discounted cash flow model
   d. Capitalization rate

9. Market Value can be determined by
   a. the NOI divided by the CAP Rate.
   b. the income less operating expenses.
   c. the NOI multiplied by the CAP rate.
   d. gross income multiplied by the CAP rate.

10. Calculate the market value, given a NOI of $90,000 and knowing that investors in this area will buy at a 9% CAP rate.
    a. $810,000
    b. $1,000,000
    c. $900,000
    d. $1,011,111

Introduction to Financial Analysis

The retail component of commercial real estate will help us illustrate several new concepts in this Chapter. You will be introduced to a form designed to organize the data REALTORS® must collect to evaluate the value of an investment property. The Annual Property Operating Data or APOD sheet utilizes all of the terms and concepts learned so far in this course. In the final section of this Chapter a typical commercial problem, centering on a neighborhood Mini-Mall, will give you the opportunity to use an Annual Property Operating Data form (APOD) to analyze a property. ■

lesson 1

Retail Terms and Lease Clauses

learning objectives

After completing this lesson, you will

■ know the concept of "anchor" tenants,

■ understand common area maintenance (CAM) charges, and

■ know the application of "tax escalation clauses."

■ Anchor Tenants

Most large shopping centers have an "anchor tenant" who usually occupies the largest store in that center. These household-name stores—often supermarkets, department stores, or national chain stores—draw people to them and consequently to the shopping center. The anchor tenant store usually does extensive advertising, which effectively benefits all the tenants of the center. The surrounding or attached stores gain free exposure to the people coming to shop at the anchor store.

In order to attract an anchor tenant, most owners reduce the rent to them but want to write a triple net lease (NNN), whereby the anchor tenant will pay its proportionate share of the full property taxes and common area maintenance charges and will be responsible for the repairs and maintenance of its own building. Often the anchor tenant will occupy half or more of the shopping center's overall square footage.

Because of the draw of this lead store to the area, other businesses will want to locate in the shopping center. They will have the advantage of the free advertising generated for the center by the anchor. The shopping center owner can now charge these smaller tenants higher rents. The owner's profit will come from these other tenants.

Traditional shopping centers have been replaced by "Power Centers" and "Mega-Malls." These centers may have several stores that could be considered anchors. In these cases, the concepts remain the same, but the anchor stores may also be paying substantial rents. The marketing strategy here is that several anchors will draw even more people to that shopping area.

■ Common Area Maintenance (CAM)

A landlord of a shopping center, strip center, office, or other type of property may provide common services to all the tenants in the building or center.

Examples of such common services are:

- Cleaning
    - Exterior—parking lot
    - Interior—hallways, lobbies, rest rooms
- Interior—office buildings, full service
- Lighting—signs, parking lot
- Landscaping
- Snow removal
- Rubbish removal
- Security
- Window washing
- Supplies—light bulbs, paper towels, etc.

The landlord's total cost of providing all these services is totaled and divided by the total square footage of the rentable area of the entire property; the result is the *per square foot common area maintenance (CAM)* charge. This is then proportionately charged to all the tenants on the square footage they occupy.

For example: Mr. Jones rents a 2,000 square foot store in a ten-store strip center that is 20,000 square foot in total size. The landlord provides common services to all the tenants, which total $60,000 per year in expenses. How much will Mr. Jones pay in common area maintenance (CAM) charges for his store?

The CAM charges are calculated by dividing the total CAM expenses, $60,000, by the total square footage of the center, 20,000 square feet; this results in a CAM charge of $3.00 per square foot (PSF) to be "passed through" to the tenants. Because Mr. Jones rents 2,000 SF, his *annual* CAM charges will be $6,000 (2,000 SF × $3.00 PSF). This is considered "additional rent" and is usually billed monthly.

Common area maintenance (CAM) charges will vary according to the services provided, the size of the property, and the geographic location. Common area maintenance (CAM) expenses to the tenant are typically in the $2.00 to $4.00 per square foot range.

■ Gross Leasable Area (GLA)

Gross leasable area (GLA) is the total square footage available for lease in a shopping center, office complex, or other type of building. The phrase is most commonly used to describe the size of large shopping centers and reflects the combined total square footage of all buildings and/or rentable floors in malls within the center.

■ Tax Escalation Clause

The *tax escalation clause* is also known as Real Estate Taxes (RET) over base, or as the tax stop. Many leases contain the tax escalation clause, which means that if the property taxes go up, the increases are proportionately passed to the tenant. The base taxes are the actual real estate taxes proportionate to the rental unit at the time of lease signing. Base taxes are paid by the landlord. Real estate taxes over base reflect tax increases that would be paid by tenants. This clause will be found in most commercial leases, including retail, office, and industrial properties.

For example: The tenants occupy a 2,000 square foot store in a shopping center with a gross leasable area (GLA) of 100,000 square feet and have a tax escalation clause in their lease. On the date the lease was signed, total real estate taxes on the shopping center were $400,000. The tenant occupies 2% of the shopping center (2,000 square feet of the 100,000 square feet center). The base taxes for this tenant are $8,000 (2% of the total taxes *on the date of lease signing* of $400,000). The landlord pays the base taxes.

Two years later, the area real estate taxes are increased by 3%. Under the tax escalation clause, the tenants must pay their proportionate share of this tax increase. This real estate tax over base is "passed through to the tenant."

The tenant's proportionate share of the 3% real estate tax increase on the shopping center is calculated as follows:

Shopping center's old real estate taxes	$400,000
Tax increase 3%	+ 12,000
Shopping center's new real estate taxes	$412,000
Tenants proportionate share of taxes, 2%	$ 8,240
Base taxes paid by landlord	$ 8,000
Tax escalation paid by tenant	$ 240

The tenant must now pay additional rent each year reflecting the additional taxes of $240.

In the example, this does not seem like a lot of money. But consider this shopping center may have 30 to 40 tenants each with tax escalation clauses. Many of these tenants may be paying tax increases for many years. Consider a ten-year lease; how many times will real estate taxes go up during that ten-year period?

With large shopping centers or office buildings having many tenants and varied leases, this additional rent can be significant and must be included in projecting income.

l e s²s o n   Annual Property Operating Data (APOD) Sheet

l e a r n i n g   o b j e c t i v e s

After completing this lesson, you will

- know how to complete an Annual Property Operating Data (APOD) sheet, and

- understand other income sources.

■ What is the APOD Form?

The Annual Property Operating Data (APOD) form was developed by the Commercial Investment Real Estate Institute, now known as the CCIM Institute, an affiliate of the National Association of REALTORS®. It, or a similar form, is used widely in the commercial/investment real estate industry. It is a checklist on which to accumulate the data needed to calculate net operating income.

The Annual Property Operating Data (APOD) sheet is also used to calculate the cash flow before taxes (CFBT), which will be explained in Chapter 6. As you look at the form, you will notice many of the terms have already been introduced in this course.

The top section of the sample form seen in Figure 5.1 records "facts" about the property—location, type of property, size, purchase price, and down payment. There is also space to enter assessment information and current or potential mortgage data.

Figure 5.1 | Sample of an Annual Property Operating Data (APOD) Form

Annual Property Operating Data

Property Name _____

Location _____

Type of Property _____

Size of Property _____ (Sq. Ft./Units)

Purpose of analysis _____

Assessed/Appraised Values _____

Land _____ _____

Improvements _____ _____

Personal Property _____

Total _____ 100%

Adjusted Basis as of: _____

Purchase Price _____

Plus Acquisiition Costs _____

Plus Loan Fees/Costs _____

Less Mortgages _____

Equals Initial Investment _____

	Balance	Periodic Pmt	Pmts/Yr	Interest	Amort Period	Loan Term
1st						
2nd						

ALL FIGURES ARE ANNUAL	$/SQ FT or $/Unit	% of GOI	COMMENTS/FOOTNOTES
1 **POTENTIAL RENTAL INCOME**			
2 Less: Vacancy & Cr. Losses			
3 **EFFECTIVE RENTAL INCOME**			
4 Plus: Other Income (collectable)			
5 **GROSS OPERATING INCOME**			
OPERATING EXPENSES:			
6 Real Estate Taxes			
7 Personal Property Taxes			
8 Property Insurance			
9 Off Site Management			
10 Payroll			
11 Expenses/Benefits			
12 Taxes/Worker's Compensation			
13 Repairs and Maintenance			
14 Utilities:			
15			
16			
17			
18			
19 Accounting and Legal			
20 Licenses/Permits			
21 Advertising			
22 Supplies			
23 Miscellaneous Contract Services:			
24			
25			
26			
27			
28			
29 **TOTAL OPERATING EXPENSES**			
30 **NET OPERATING INCOME**			
31 Less: Annual Debt Service			
32 Less: Participation Payments			
33 Less: Leasing Commissions			
34 Less: Funded Reserves			
35 **CASH FLOW BEFORE TAXES**			

Authored by Gary G. Tharp, CCIM   Copyright© 2002 by the CCIM Institute   Reprinted with Permission

The statements and figures herein, while not guaranteed, are secured from sources we believe authoritative.

Prepared for: _____

Prepared by: _____

The remainder of the form is numbered 1 through 35. Most of this information may be supplied by the current property owner and should eventually be verified by the potential buyer. Each line calls for a numeric value; some entries require a calculation. *Important note: All figures entered on the Annual Property Operating Data Form must be annual totals.*

On the right side of the form is a section headed Comments/Footnotes. Here you might indicate a conversion note, e.g., if you converted a monthly or per square foot cost to an annual charge. For example, rubbish removal is $500 per month. Your entry in line 23, Miscellaneous Contract Services, would indicate the annual expense of $6,000. Under Comments/Footnotes you would show: "$500 per month × 12 months = $6,000 annual cost."

■ Line-by-Line Review

Following is a review of the entries line by line. Remember the APOD is a checklist: *You will not always have an entry on every line.*

1. Potential Rental Income (PRI)

   This reflects the income from the property's entire rentable square footage, even if some space is currently unoccupied. You project income for any unoccupied space. The potential rental income (PRI) is the total annual income expected from rent. This would include the basic rent roll plus any additional rent collected from tax escalations and common area maintenance (CAM) charges.

2. Less: Vacancy & Credit Losses

   A percentage is used as the basis for this contingency expense. Calculate that percentage of the total income on line 1 and enter the dollar result on line 2.

3. Effective Rental Income

   This is a subtotal line. Subtract line 2 from line 1.

4. Plus: Other Income (collectable)

   This is other income to the building or property that is not affected by tenants. Some examples would be:

   - On the roof of an office building—antennas, satellite dishes, etc.
   - Billboards
   - Vending machines, pay phones
   - In an apartment building—laundry room, garage rental

5. Gross Operating Income

   This line totals the income portion of the form. Add together lines 3 and 4.

The next portion of the form (lines 6 through 29) are the Operating Expenses for the property. Record only expenses paid by the owner here; anything paid by tenants is not included in this analysis. The form lists the most common expense categories. You may not have an entry for all items listed, and you may have expenses that are not listed. What is important is that all the expenses are accounted for. Modify the form as needed. *Convert all expenses to annual cost.*

6. Real Estate Taxes

7. Personal Property Taxes

   Depending on which state the property is located in, enter the appropriate taxes that are paid by the owner of the property.

8. Property Insurance

   Enter annual insurance costs.

9. Off-Site Management

   Often a property management firm of a real estate brokerage company is hired to manage the building or property. This could involve many different levels of responsibilities for different fees. Generally, compensation is in the form of a percentage of the rental income. *Caution: This compensation could be a percentage of gross rent, net rent, actual income; the basis must be defined.* If the building has off-site management, unless otherwise specified, calculate the percentage fee based on "base rent roll" included in the Potential Rental Income (line 1) and insert the dollar figure in line 9.

10. Payroll

11. Expenses/Benefits

12. Taxes/Worker's Compensation

   If employees are hired by the property owner, complete lines 10, 11, and 12, with the actual annual expenses. This could include maintenance personnel, security officers and, in apartment buildings, the superintendent or others.

13. Repairs and Maintenance

   This is a contingency fund for "catastrophic" events that would require immediate repair or replacement. Examples are roof repairs or heating, ventilating and air-conditioning (HVAC) problems that require system replacement. This expense is most often calculated as a percentage of the building's income, but it could also be a fixed dollar amount. *Caution: When using a percentage, determine if the owner does the calculation based on the potential rental income (line 1) or the gross operating income (line 5).*

   As a guideline to selecting a percentage, consider the age and condition of the building(s) and know what responsibilities the owner has for repair and maintenance under the leases. As a rule of thumb, repair and maintenance expenses are usually in the range of 5 percent to 10 percent of the gross operating income of the property.

14–18. Utilities

   These expenses are only for the utilities paid by the owner.

19. Accounting and Legal

20. Licenses/Permits

21. Advertising

22. Supplies

23–28. Miscellaneous Contract Services

   Enter any of these expenses on an annual cost basis.

   Regular and routine services are listed here. These could be services that are billed to the tenants under common area maintenance (CAM) charges. Examples are rubbish collection, cleaning, window washing, etc. Be sure to enter the annual cost of these expenses.

29. Total Operating Expenses

   Total all of the owner's operating expenses.

30. Net Operating Income

   The Gross Operating Income (line 5) less the Total Operating Expenses (line 29) equals the Net Operating Income. Calculate and enter on line 30.

31–35. The final lines, 31 through 35, of the Annual Property Operating Data (APOD) form will be discussed in Chapter 6.

les**3**on

APOD Case Study: Mini-Mall

learning objectives

After completing this lesson, you will have

- gained experience calculating variable rental incomes,
- performed annual conversions of operating expenses,
- experienced using the Annual Property Operating Data (APOD) sheet for analysis, and
- calculated market value from raw data.

case study

Mountain View Mini-Mall APOD

Our client owns a neighborhood strip center called the Mountain View Mini-Mall consisting of six stores with a gross leasable area (GLA) of 10,000 SF. The site is 40,000 SF. The rent roll is as follows:

Store	Size (SF)	Rent (PSF)
Restaurant	1,500	$15
Dry cleaner	1,500	$15
Video (2 storefronts)	3,000	$18
Stationery shop	2,000	$18
Real estate agent	2,000	$16

All tenants pay additional rent of $1.00 per square foot (PSF) common area maintenance (CAM) charges.

The landlord's expenses are as follows:

Parking lot cleaning	per week	$25
Landscaping	per year	$420
Electricity—Sign	per month	$50
Insurance	per year	$6,500
Snow removal	per year	$500
Rubbish removal	per month	$150
Accountant	per year	$1,200
Property taxes	per year	$52,000

The landlord rarely has vacancies but uses a 5% vacancy contingency in his financial statements. He pays a real estate broker 4% of his base rent roll to manage the center. The owner puts $10,000 a year into an emergency repair and maintenance fund. There are no other expenses.

■ Case Study Problem

Analyze the property using the Annual Property Operating Data (APOD) form (on page 39) and develop a market value for the Mountain View Mini-Mall based on offering a 12% return to the buyer. Give no consideration to debt service in this exercise.

Solution Mountain View Mini-Mall Annual Property Operating Data (APOD) Form

To solve this Case Study, break the problem down into steps. There are five steps involved in the solution.

STEP 1

Calculate the potential rental income

Potential rental income includes all possible income whether the space is occupied or not. In this problem, all the spaces are occupied. Using the Annual Property Operating Data (APOD) form as a checklist, allow: line 1 to ask: What is the potential rental income?

To find the potential rental income, you must calculate each tenant's rent to the annual income and then total all the tenant's income.

To calculate the annual rent for each tenant, multiply the square footage occupied times the rent per square foot, for example, Restaurant Tenant: 1,500 SF × $15PSF = $22,500 annual rent

Rent Roll Calculations

Store	SF	x	Base Rent ($ PSF)	=	Annual Rent ($)
Restaurant	1,500	×	15.	=	22,500
Dry cleaner	1,500	×	15.	=	22,500
Video store	3,000	×	18.	=	54,000
Stationary store	2,000	×	18.	=	36,000
Real estate office	2,000	×	16.	=	32,000
Total Rent Roll	10,000			=	167,000

Add to the Total Rent Roll any additional rent paid by the tenants.

In this problem, the building owner charges the tenants additional rent for common area maintenance (CAM) of $1 PSF. The total building size is 10,000 SF. Therefore: 10,000 SF × $1.00 PSF CAM = $10,000 annual CAM income. Add this figure to the base rent roll total to determine the potential rental income: $167,000 + $10,000 = $177,000. The potential rental income is $177,000; enter this figure on line 1, Potential Rental Income, of the form.

Solution *(continued)*

STEP 2

Analyze all other income and adjustments to income - solve for gross operating income (GOI). (Refer to page 47 for solution.)

Review the other income section lines on the form (page 39). Let each line of the checklist ask you a question.

Line 2—What are the Vacancy and Credit Losses?

The problem tells us to use 5% vacancy contingency. This is an adjustment to the potential rental income.

Potential Rental Income	$177,000
Multiplied by 5%	× .05
Vacancy and Credit Losses	$ 8,850

Enter $8,850 on line 2, Less: Vacancy & Credit Losses, of the APOD form.

Line 3—Effective Rental Income

When we subtract the dollar amount on line 2 from line 1, we know the effective rental income.

Total Rental Income	$ 177,000
Less: Vacancy & Credit Losses	− $ 8,850
Effective Rental Income	$ 168,150

Enter $168,150 on line 3 of the form.

Line 4—Poses the question: Is there any "other income collectable"? In this problem, there is none—leave line 4 of the form blank.

Line 5—Gross Operating Income

Because there is no additional income in this problem on line 4, the effective rental income will be the same as the gross operating income. Enter $168,150 on line 6 of the form.

STEP 3

Calculate the owner's operating expenses

Reread the problem and use the form as a checklist to enter the various expenses. Be sure to convert all figures to annual expenses. Then total all the operating expenses. In this case, the total operating expenses are $81,000, calculated as follows:

Real estate taxes (line 6)	$ 52,000
Insurance (line 8)	$ 6,500
Off-site management (line 9)	$ 6,680

The problem stated: The owner "...pays a real estate broker 4% of his *base rent roll* to manage the center." This is the off-site management expense. The base rent roll is the potential rental income.

The expense amount was calculated by multiplying the base rent roll by 4%, i.e., $167,000 × .04 = $6,680.

Solution *(continued)*

You may be questioning why the income from the common area maintenance (CAM) charges is not included; this income is generally considered a "pass through" of expenses. For example, the income from common area maintenance (CAM) charges would be used to pay for the "contract services" that the charges are based upon. Tax escalations pay part of the tax bill. The landlord never benefits from this money.

Line 13—Repairs and Maintenance

Repairs and maintenance is a contingency expense that is usually applied as a percentage of the rental income. But, in some cases, a fixed figure is used. In this case it is $10,000.

As real estate practitioners, we must question the "reality" of a fixed figure when it is used. If you recall, we previously noted that the typical percentage used in calculating repair and maintenance contingency expense is between 5% and 10%. As a comparison, if *in this problem* we relate the fixed figure used to the gross operating income (GOI) we find it reflects 6%, an acceptable percentage within the bounds of our "reality" range. (The repair and maintenance fixed figure is divided by the gross operating income: $10,000 ÷ $168,150 = .059 or 6%.)

Lines 14–18—Utilities

Electric	$600

This requires a conversion from a monthly charge of $50 to an annual expense: $50 per month × 12 months = $600 annual expense.

Line 19—Accounting and Legal $1,200

Lines 24-28—Contract Services

Cleaning	$1,300

Cleaning is based on $25 per week times 52 weeks.

Landscaping	$420
Snow Removal	$500
Rubbish Removal	$1,800

Rubbish removal is based on $150 per month times 12 months

Added together, the Total Operating Expenses are: $81,000

The $81,000 is entered on line 29 of the form.

STEP 4

Calculate the Net Operating Income (NOI)

The net operating income (NOI) is the result of subtracting the Total Operating Expenses (line 29) from the Gross Operating Income (line 5).

Gross Operating Income	$168,150
Less: Operating Expenses	– 81,000
Net Operating Income	$ 87,150

Enter the NOI on line 30 of the form.

A completed form follows in Figure 5.2 on page 47.

Solution (continued)

STEP 5

Calculate the market value of the Mountain View Mini-Mall

The problem asks that we calculate the "Market Value" of the property based on offering a 12% return on the buyer's investment. This is basically the same as a building owner asking: What is my building worth? Given that we know what returns, capitalization rates (CAP rates), investors expect in our areas, with the net operating income (NOI) we can now calculate market value or asking price.

To solve this problem for market value, we apply the CAP rate formula previously learned.

Net Operating Income (NOI)	$87,150
Capitalization Rate (CAP rate)	12%
NOI ÷ CAP rate = Value	
87,150 ÷ .12 = 726,250	
Market Value	$726,250

You have now learned to analyze a property with the help of an Annual Property Operating Data (APOD) form, and have a factual basis on which to answer the client's question, "What is my property worth?"

Figure 5.2 | Sample of a Completed Annual Property Operating Data (APOD) Form

Annual Property Operating Data

Property Name: Mini Mall

Location: _____

Type of Property: Retail Srip

Size of Property: 10,000 SF/6 (Sq. Ft./Units)

Purpose of analysis: _____

Assessed/Appraised Values

Land	_____	_____
Improvements	_____	_____
Personal Property	_____	_____
Total	_____	100%

Adjusted Basis as of: _____

Purchase Price: _____
Plus Acquisiition Costs: _____
Plus Loan Fees/Costs: _____
Less Mortgages: _____
Equals Initial Investment: _____

	Balance	Periodic Pmt	Pmts/Yr	Interest	Amort Period	Loan Term
1st	_____	_____	12	_____	_____	_____
2nd	_____	_____	12	_____	_____	_____

ALL FIGURES ARE ANNUAL	$/SQ FT or $/Unit	% of GOI			COMMENTS/FOOTNOTES
1 **POTENTIAL RENTAL INCOME**	_____			177,000	Base Rent $167,000 + $10,000 CAM
2 Less: Vacancy & Cr. Losses		(5% of PRI)		8,850	
3 **EFFECTIVE RENTAL INCOME**				168,150	
4 Plus: Other Income (collectable)	_____				
5 **GROSS OPERATING INCOME**				168,150	
OPERATING EXPENSES:					
6 Real Estate Taxes			52,000		
7 Personal Property Taxes					
8 Property Insurance			6,500		
9 Off Site Management			6,680		4% of Base Rent $167,000
10 Payroll					
11 Expenses/Benefits					
12 Taxes/Worker's Compensation					
13 Repairs and Maintenance			10,000		
14 Utilities:					
Electric			600		$50 month (X12)
16					
17					
18					
19 Accounting and Legal			1,200		
20 Licenses/Permits					
21 Advertising					
22 Supplies					
23 Miscellaneous Contract Services:					
24 Cleaning			1,300		$25 week (X52)
25 Landscaping			420		
26			500		
27			1,800		$150 month (X12)
28					
29 TOTAL OPERATING EXPENSES				81,000	
30 **NET OPERATING INCOME**				87,150	
31 Less: Annual Debt Service					
32 Less: Participation Payments					
33 Less: Leasing Commissions					
34 Less: Funded Reserves					
35 **CASH FLOW BEFORE TAXES**					

Prepared for: _____

Prepared by: _____

■ Chapter 5 Review Questions

1. A store that draws people to a shopping center is known as the
   a. lead store.
   b. credit tenant.
   c. anchor tenant.
   d. None of the above

2. What would be a CAM charge?
   a. Legal expenses
   b. Rubbish removal
   c. Debt service
   d. Property taxes

3. A tax escalation clause could cause
   a. additional rent.
   b. less rent.
   c. increased taxes.
   d. decreased taxes.

4. The total square footage available for lease in a shopping center is known as
   a. CAM.
   b. RET.
   c. PSF.
   d. GLA.

5. What item would be affected by vacancy?
   a. Vending machines
   b. Roof antennas
   c. CAM charges
   d. Pay phones

6. On the APOD form, what is usually calculated as a percentage?
   a. Vacancy and credit losses
   b. Off-site management
   c. Repair and maintenance
   d. All of the above

7. Using the APOD form, the NOI is determined by subtracting the total operating expenses from what?
   a. Potential rental income
   b. Gross operating income
   c. Effective rental income
   d. Annual debt service

8. On the APOD form, "Other Income (not affected by vacancy)" sources may include?
   a. Antennas on the roof
   b. Laundry room income from an apartment house
   c. Billboards on the property
   d. All of the above

9. All dollar figures entered on the APOD form reflect
   a. monthly totals.
   b annual totals.
   c. payment basis used (per week, per month, etc.).
   d. best monthly estimates available.

10. The primary purpose of an APOD form is to
    a. serve as a checklist to gather and organize data.
    b. determine the property's overall value.
    c. determine market value of a building.
    d. define all possible expenses.

The Value of Investments

overview

Sometimes an investor can make more money by using "other people's money" as part of the investment strategy. Other people's money could simply be a bank mortgage or may involve gathering together a group of other investors, "partners," for the project.

There are many different terms used to describe the value of an investment to the owner or to a potential purchaser. ■

learning objectives

After completing this lesson, you will

■ know the definition of rate of return,

■ learn to calculate cash flow before taxes (CFBT),

■ learn to calculate cash on cash returns,

■ realize the impact of leveraging on the cash on cash return, and

■ understand the concept of internal rate of return (IRR).

In Chapter 4, we looked at the capitalization rate (CAP rate) as an investor's desired "profit percentage" that is used to project the property value.

This Chapter will focus primarily on the current owner, work with the actual sale prices of a property, and determine existing rates of return.

It is necessary to define the key terms that will be used.

■ Key Investment Terms

Rate of Return—The percentage return on each dollar invested. Also known as the **yield.**

Leverage—The use of borrowed funds to finance a portion of the cost of an investment. Typically this is in the form of a **mortgage** on the property. The **annual** expense of a mortgage including principal and interest is referred to as annual **debt service.**

Initial investment—This is the **down payment.** The sales price plus acquisition costs less the amount of the mortgage loan is the down payment.

Cash flow before taxes (CFBT)—The net operating income (NOI) less the annual debt service equals cash flow before taxes (CFBT).

Equity—The value of one's interest in the property, consisting of fair market value less any outstanding debt or other encumbrances. Equity generally increases as the mortgage balance decreases.

Cash on cash return—A simple return measure. Calculated as cash flow before taxes (CFBT) divided by the initial investment or down payment.

Internal Rate of Return (IRR)—This is a calculation that covers the entire life of the investment and in essence shows the "average" annual return for the entire holding period. This mathematically complex calculation is the discount rate when the present value of future cash flows is exactly equal to the initial capital investment.

Internal rate of return (IRR) is covered in advanced investment courses. It is only mentioned here so the student is aware that there are other methods used by investors to evaluate investment properties.

■ Comparison of Investment Methods

All Cash Purchase

In the final problem in Chapter 5 we determined, based on a 12% capitalization rate (CAP rate), the market value of the six-store strip center, known as the Mountain View Mini-Mall, to be $726,250.

If an investor bought the property for $726,250, all cash, they would have after the first year a 12% *return on investment (ROI)* of $87,150 net operating expenses (NOI) before taxes.

Leveraged Purchase

If the buyer of the Mini-Mall financed the purchase by obtaining a bank mortgage, *leveraging* the purchase, what would be the buyer's *cash on cash return?*

To determine this, it is necessary to apply the definitions learned earlier in this Chapter and to know the terms of the bank mortgage.

The relevant formulas are as follows:

> **Cash Flow Before Taxes = Net Operating Income – Annual Debt Service**
>
> **Cash on Cash = Cash Flow Before Taxes ÷ Initial Investment**

In order to determine cash on cash returns, we must first calculate the cash flow before taxes (CFBT). From our Mini-Mall problem we know the following:

Sales Price	$726,250
Net Operating Income (NOI)	$87,150

For purposes of this comparison, we will make the following mortgage assumptions: 15-year term, 7.5% interest, and 25% down payment, with monthly payments. Based on these assumptions, the "annual debt service" can be calculated as follows:

Sales Price	$726,250
Down Payment (25%)	$181,562
Mortgage Amount	$544,688
Annual Debt Service	$60,592

We now have all of the figures required to calculate the cash on cash return.

Solution – Calculating Mountain View Mini-Mall Cash on Cash Return

STEP 1

Calculate the cash flow before taxes (CFBT)

Net Operating Income (NOI)	$87,150
Minus: Annual Debt Service	– 60,592
Cash Flow Before Taxes (CFBT)	$26,558

STEP 2

Calculate the cash on cash return

CFBT ÷ Initial Investment = Cash on Cash Return

$26,558 (CFBT) ÷ $181,562 (Initial Investment) = .1463 (14.6%) Cash on Cash Return

---

In this case, *leveraging* increased the investor's return from 12% return on investment (ROI) in the all-cash purchase example, to 14.6% cash on cash return. In addition, by leveraging this purchase, the investor would still have $544,688 from his original cash to make other investments.

Hint: The interest rate and terms of the mortgage will affect the cash on cash return. This could in some cases make the all-cash purchase return on investment (ROI) a higher overall return. Potential investment returns should be evaluated both ways.

■ Investor Strategies

Each investor has his or her own goals with investment properties. Different strategies may cause investors to focus on certain criteria for their purchases, such as the following:

- **Stability**—Stable building, fully rented, reasonable return
- **Potential**—Building requires "upgrading"—future potential for a higher return
- **Flipping**—Buy depressed and then fix up and sell quickly, or flip, at profit
- **Upside Potential**—Good building , old leases, low current rents, replace tenants
- **Holder**—Buys for the long term, never sells.

Investors have many considerations and goals in choosing the properties they buy. As a broker, discuss with your investor clients their particular selection strategy; it will help you service them better.

Most investors seek immediate cash flow profits from their properties. But some investors are more concerned that they never have to add money to their investment as a result of vacancy and the consequent lack of income. As an example, investor A buys buildings with 25 percent down and seeks 15-year mortgages. His only criteria is to be sure the net operating income (NOI) is sufficient to pay the debt service on the buildings. In so doing, his required rents to break even are usually below market and he literally never has any vacancies in his buildings.

In 15 years, when he retires, all his mortgages will start to be paid off and the income from his buildings will be his retirement. This will allow him to live comfortably on his income and pass the ownership of the buildings to his family.

Know the goals of your investors; it will help you find the right property for them.

■ Chapter 6 Review Questions

1. Leveraging is
   a. a guarantee of a higher yield.
   b. the use of borrowed funds to finance a portion of the cost of an investment.
   c. NOI less the annual debt service.
   d. the fair market value less any outstanding debt or encumbrances.

2. The method to determine the cash on cash return is to
   a. subtract the debt service from the NOI.
   b. divide the cash flow before taxes by the initial investment.
   c. subtract the down payment from the sales price.
   d. divide the initial investment by the ROI.

3. The net operating income less the annual debt service is
   a. investment return.
   b. cash on cash.
   c. cash flow before taxes.
   d. the equity.

4. A calculation that considers the entire life of the investment is
   a. cash on cash return.
   b. return on investment.
   c. leveraging.
   d. internal rate of return.

5. The desired profit percentage of an investor is called
   a. CAP rate.
   b. ROI.
   c. NOI.
   d. CFBT.

6. The annual debt service figure is necessary to calculate
   a. initial investment
   b. ROI
   c. yield
   d. cash flow before taxes

7. Leveraging
   a. always increases the return on an investment.
   b. never effects the return on an investment.
   c. requires the CAP rate for calculation.
   d. may increase returns on investments depending upon rates and terms of the financing.

8. A property has an NOI of $67,500, and an investor offers $450,000, all cash, to purchase it. What ROI is that investor expecting?
   a. 6.67%
   b. 15%
   c. 12.5%
   d. None of the above

9. A property has an NOI of $67,500, and an investor offers $450,000 to purchase it with a down payment of $100,000. The annual debt service for the mortgage is $38,934. What is the buyer's anticipated cash-on-cash return?
   a. 39%
   b. 29%
   c. 6%
   d. 8%

10. If in problem 9 the down payment was increased to $200,000, the Cash on Cash Return would
    a. increase.
    b. decrease.
    c. remain the same.
    d. become zero.

7

Forecasting Cash Flows

This chapter consists of four lessons that analyze a small office building. The analysis begins with the current year, expands to a five-year review and looks at value from both the owner's and buyer's perspective. You will learn to project the future income of properties, its effect on value, and how investors "think."

The first three lessons, Lesson 1–Current Year Analysis, Lesson 2–The Spreadsheet, and Lesson 3–Returns on Investments, are all used to answer the office building problem in the case study. ■

case study   Mr. Smith's Small Office Building

Mr. Smith, the client in this case study, owns a building and wants to put it on the market for sale. His question is: *"What is my building worth?"*

To answer this question, it will be necessary to create an Annual Property Operating Data (APOD) sheet for year one and make adjustments to the income and expenses for the next four years. Creating current and projected net operating incomes (NOI) will give us a basis for value.

If existing debt service is factored in, cash on cash returns can be determined over the five-year period, showing value from the owner's point of view.

This exercise continues through the entire Chapter and involves many of the concepts already learned in this course. It is a real world problem, typical of what commercial and investment practitioners do every day.

■ Case Study Problem

It is December of the current year. Mr. Smith called you and said he wanted to sell his office building. He asked you to stop by and tell him what it was worth.

You advised him that before you could do that, you would need a summary of the leases (or copies of the actual leases) and all the expenses for the building. In addition, he would need to answer certain questions for you. An interview is arranged; you meet and gather the data you need for evaluation. A synopsis of the relevant facts is found below.

Building Description

The owner's building has the following features:

- It is a three story, Class B, office building with elevator.
- Each floor has a gross leasable area of 2,500 square feet.
- There is a 1,200 square foot leasable area in the lower level, which is presently the only vacancy in the building.
- Roof space is leased to a phone company for an antenna.

The gross square footage leased to each tenant and their lease terms follow:

Tenant	SF	Lease Start	Lease End	Annual Escalations	Current Rent ($ PSF)
A	2,500	Jan., 10 years ago	Dec., current year	2%	$14
B	1,250	Jan., 4 years ago	Dec., 6 yrs. from now	3%	$18
C	1,250	Jan., 3 years ago	Dec., 7 yrs. from now	4%	$19
D	1,500	Jan., 2 years ago	Dec., 13 yrs. from now	10% every 5 years	$19
E	1,000	Jan., 1 year ago	Dec., 9 yrs. from now	3%	$20
F	1,200		Vacant (Projected Rent)		$10

Other Building Considerations

Keep in mind the following when doing the analysis of the building:

- There is an agreement that allows a phone company to have a relay antenna on the roof for a fee of $500 per month.
- The owner uses 7% as a vacancy adjustment, 5% for repair contingency based on the Gross Operating Income (GOI) and manages the building himself.
- Taxes are presently $50,000 per year but have just been reduced. The tax reductions are effective as follows: a reduction of $2,500 in two years, a further reduction of $2,500 in the year after that.
- All other operating expenses combine to $20,000 presently and are expected to increase at a rate of 3% per year.
- The current owner bought the building five years ago for $500,000. He paid $125,000 cash down and financed $375,000 at 9% interest (fixed rate) for 15 years. Annual mortgage payments are $45,642.

lesson 1   Current Year Analysis

learning objectives

After completing this lesson, you will

■ understand the relevant components required for cash flow analysis,

■ gain experience using the Annual Property Operating Data (APOD) form, and

■ gain a greater understanding of the effects of leveraging.

■ Forecasting Cash Flows

To properly present an investment opportunity for a property with an upside potential, we must project the cash flow for future years. This is generally done with a five-year analysis, but it could be done for a longer period, if appropriate.

Small Office Building Problem Part A

To begin analyzing the office building, complete an Annual Property Operating Data (APOD) form and determine the cash on cash return on the building.

Hint: Information has been provided that you do not need for this part of the problem. You are only concerned in this part with the current year's income and expenses. Do the problem in steps using the Annual Property Operating Data (APOD) form as a checklist. See Figure 7.1.

Figure 7.1 | Sample Annual Property Operating Data (APOD) Form

Annual Property Operating Data

Property Name _____

Location _____

Type of Property _____

Size of Property _____ (Sq. Ft./Units)

Purpose of analysis _____

Assessed/Appraised Values

Land _____

Improvements _____

Personal Property _____

Total _____ 100%

Adjusted Basis as of: _____

Purchase Price _____

Plus Acquisiition Costs _____

Plus Loan Fees/Costs _____

Less Mortgages _____

Equals Initial Investment _____

	Balance	Periodic Pmt	Pmts/Yr	Interest	Amort Period	Loan Term
1st						
2nd						

ALL FIGURES ARE ANNUAL	$/SQ FT or $/Unit	% of GOI		COMMENTS/FOOTNOTES
1 **POTENTIAL RENTAL INCOME**				
2 Less: Vacancy & Cr. Losses				
3 **EFFECTIVE RENTAL INCOME**				
4 Plus: Other Income (collectable)				
5 **GROSS OPERATING INCOME**				
OPERATING EXPENSES:				
6 Real Estate Taxes				
7 Personal Property Taxes				
8 Property Insurance				
9 Off Site Management				
10 Payroll				
11 Expenses/Benefits				
12 Taxes/Worker's Compensation				
13 Repairs and Maintenance				
14 Utilities:				
15				
16				
17				
18				
19 Accounting and Legal				
20 Licenses/Permits				
21 Advertising				
22 Supplies				
23 Miscellaneous Contract Services:				
24				
25				
26				
27				
28				
29 TOTAL OPERATING EXPENSES				
30 **NET OPERATING INCOME**				
31 Less: Annual Debt Service				
32 Less: Participation Payments				
33 Less: Leasing Commissions				
34 Less: Funded Reserves				
35 **CASH FLOW BEFORE TAXES**				

Authored by Gary G. Tharp, CCIM   Copyright© 2002 by the CCIM Institute   Reprinted with Permission

The statements and figures herein, while not guaranteed, are secured from sources we believe authoritative.

Prepared for: _____

Prepared by: _____

Solution Small Office Building Problem Part A

STEP 1

Complete the top portion of the Annual Property Operating Data (APOD) Form

Based on the facts stated in the problem, the following information should be entered:

Type of Property	Office Building Class B
Size of Property	8,700 SF / 6 Units
Purchase Price	$500,000
Down Payment	$125,000
Existing Mortgage and Terms	Payment: $45,642 per year, Interest: 9%, Term: 15 years

STEP 2

Determine the Current Rent Roll and the Potential Rental Income (PRI)—Line 1.

The current rent roll is determined by first multiplying each tenant's gross square footage (GSF) times the rent per square foot (PSF) resulting in each tenant's annual rent. All the tenants' incomes are then added together to equal the Total Potential Rental Income. All rentable space is considered whether occupied or not.

Tenant	SF	Rent ($ PSF)	Annual Rent ($)
A	2,500	14	35,000
B	1,250	18	22,500
C	1,250	19	23,700
D	1,500	19	28,500
E	1,000	20	20,000
F (Projected)	1,200	10	12,000
Total Rent Roll			141,750

Next, any additional rent collected by the landlord (i.e., common area maintenance (CAM) charges, tax escalations, etc.) is added to the rent roll. The total is the potential rental income (PRI). In this problem, no additional rent is charged.

STEP 3

Complete the Other Income —lines 2 through 5

Refer to line 2 which calls for calculating Vacancy & Credit Losses; in this problem the owner uses 7% as a vacancy contingency. Take 7% of the potential rental income (PRI) (line 1) to determine the Vacancy Adjustment: $141,750 × .07 = $9,922.50, rounded to $9,923.

Line 3, "Effective Rental Income" results from subtracting the dollar amount of the Vacancy Adjustment from the total rental income: $141,750 – $9,923 = $131,827.

Line 4, asks if there is any "Other Income" collectable? In this case there is income from the roof antenna in the amount to $500 per month. This must be converted to an annual figure. $500 × 12 = $6,000.

Line 5, is the "Gross Operating Income"; total the Effective Rental Income (line 3) and Other Income (line 4) to determine this: $131,827 + $6,000 = $137,827.

STEP 4

Enter the Operating Expenses —Line 29

In this problem, there are only three expenses:

Line 6, Real Estate Taxes = $50,000.

Line 13, Repairs and Maintenance = $6,891.
   The Repairs and Maintenance are stated by the owner to be 5% of the gross operating income (GOI): $137,827 × .05 = $6,891.

Line 23, Miscellaneous Contract Expenses, used for "all other expenses" = $20,000.

Line 29, Total Operating Expenses, determined by adding all the expenses in lines 6, 13, and 23 = $76,891.

STEP 5

Determine the Net Operating Income (NOI)

The Gross Operating Income (GOI) minus the Total Operating Expenses (TOE) equals the net operating income (NOI).

$$\$137,827 \text{ (GOI)} - \$76,891 \text{ (TOE)} = \$60,936 \text{ (NOI)}$$

This figure should be entered on line 30 of the form.

STEP 6

Determine the Cash Flow Before Taxes (CFBT)

Line 31, Annual Debt Service (i.e., annual mortgage payment) = $45,642.

The Cash Flow Before Taxes (CFBT) is determined by subtracting the Annual Debt Service from the Net Operating income (NOI). $60,936 (NOI) – $45,642 (Debt Service) = $15,294 (CFBT). This figure is entered on line 35.

A sample completed Annual Property Operating Data (APOD) form follows in Figure 7.3.

STEP 7

Determine the Cash on Cash Return

The cash on cash return is equal to the cash flow before taxes (CFBT) divided by the initial investment. The initial investment is the down payment.

$$\text{Cash on Cash Return} = \text{CFBT} \div \text{Initial Investment}$$

$15,294 (CFBT) ÷ $125,000 (Initial Investment) = .1224 or 12.24% Cash on Cash Return

Figure 7.2 | Completed Annual Property Operating Data (APOD) form

Annual Property Operating Data

Property Name _____

Location _____

Type of Property ___Office Building Class B___

Size of Property ___8,700 SF/6 U___ (Sq. Ft./Units)

Purpose of analysis _____

Assessed/Appraised Values ____

Land		
Improvements		
Personal Property		
Total		100%

Adjusted Basis as of: ____ $500,000

Purchase Price _____ 500,000

Plus Acquisiition Costs _____

Plus Loan Fees/Costs _____

Less Mortgages _____ 375,000

Equals Initial Investment _____ 125,000

	Balance	Periodic Pmt	Pmts/Yr	Interest	Amort Period	Loan Term
1st		$45,642	12	9.%		15 yrs
2nd			12			

ALL FIGURES ARE ANNUAL	$/SQ FT or $/Unit	% of GOI		COMMENTS/FOOTNOTES
1 POTENTIAL RENTAL INCOME			141,750	
2 Less: Vacancy & Cr. Losses			9,923	141,750 X .07 = 9,922.50
3 EFFECTIVE RENTAL INCOME			131,827	
4 Plus: Other Income (collectable)			6,000	500 X 12 = 6,000
5 GROSS OPERATING INCOME			137,827	
OPERATING EXPENSES:				
6 Real Estate Taxes			50,000	
7 Personal Property Taxes				
8 Property Insurance				
9 Off Site Management				
10 Payroll				
11 Expenses/Benefits				
12 Taxes/Worker's Compensation				
13 Repairs and Maintenance			6,891	137,827 X .05 = 6,891
14 Utilities:				
Electric				
16				
17				
18				
19 Accounting and Legal				
20 Licenses/Permits				
21 Advertising				
22 Supplies				
23 Miscellaneous Contract Services:				
24 All Other Expenses			20,000	
25				
26				
27				
28				
29 TOTAL OPERATING EXPENSES			76,891	
30 NET OPERATING INCOME			60,936	
31 Less: Annual Debt Service			45,642	
32 Less: Participation Payments				
33 Less: Leasing Commissions				
34 Less: Funded Reserves				
35 CASH FLOW BEFORE TAXES			$15,294	

Authored by Gary G. Tharp, CCIM   Copyright© 2002 by the CCIM Institute   Reprinted with Permission

The statements and figures herein, while not guaranteed, are secured from sources we believe authoritative.

Prepared for: _____

Prepared by: _____

As seen in Figure 7.2, the owner enjoys a 12.24 percent return on the investment today, five years after the purchase. One would have expected a higher rate of return after holding a property for five years. The problem with the bottom line on this investment is largely caused by the 9 percent interest rate of the mortgage. If you recall the leveraging example in Chapter 6, leveraging brought the cash on cash return up to 14 percent as opposed to an all-cash purchase of 12 percent. But, the interest rate was 7.5 percent. It is important to note that, based upon the economy and prevailing interest rates, the effects of leveraging on the bottom line—the profit of the investment—will vary.

The problem stated that the investor bought the building five years ago. If he had bought the building for all cash for $500,000, what would his return be today? Using the capitalization rate (CAP rate) formula we can determine this.

Net Operating Income ÷ Value (Purchase Price) = Capitalization Rate

$60,936 (NOI) ÷ $500,000 (Value) = .1219 or 12.19% CAP rate

At this time, without debt servicing, the property would be giving the owner a 12 percent-plus return on the investment, about the same as leveraging at the higher interest rate. However, by leveraging the property, the cash outlay—down payment—at the time of the purchase was $125,000. Assuming the current owner had $500,000 to spend when he bought the building, by leveraging he would have been able to acquire other investments. He may have accepted a lower rate of return on some, like this property, that he believed had good upside potential.

l e s s o n   The Spreadsheet

l e a r n i n g   o b j e c t i v e s

After completing this lesson, you will

- understand the impact of up-side events,

- know how to calculate rent escalations, and

- be able to develop five year property projections.

In order to give a potential buyer a clear picture of a purchase opportunity including return on investment and up-side potential, it is often necessary to do a five-year or longer forecast of cash flows. In essence, Annual Property Operating Data (APOD) forms for five years, but rather than use that form a "spreadsheet" is created.

■ Small Office Building Problem Part B

Create a five-year spreadsheet showing the cash flow before taxes (CFBT) on the office building.

Part B of the problem is done in two steps, the first being to develop the potential rental income (PRI) for each year. To accomplish this, each individual lease must be examined and the rent escalations (increases) for each year calculated.

A spreadsheet is necessary to record the potential rental income (PRI) for each year. From the solution to Part A of the problem, the current year's rent roll is known. It has been entered under "Current Year" on the following spreadsheet. Complete the spreadsheet by adding the appropriate rent increases to each tenant anticipated annual rent.

Small Office Building Problem Part B

STEP 1

Calculate potential rental income for each year

Tenant	Current Year	Year 2	Year 3	Year 4	Year 5
A	$35,000	_____	_____	_____	_____
B	$22,500	_____	_____	_____	_____
C	$23,750	_____	_____	_____	_____
D	$28,500	_____	_____	_____	_____
E	$20,000	_____	_____	_____	_____
F	$12,000	_____	_____	_____	_____
Total	$141,750	_____	_____	_____	_____

The lease terms and increases must now be examined; they are reprinted below:

Tenant	SF	Lease Start	Lease End	Annual Escalations	Current Rent ($ PSF)
A	2,500	Jan., 10 years ago	Dec., current year	2%	14
B	1,250	Jan., 4 years ago	Dec., 6 yrs. from now	3%	18
C	1,250	Jan., 3 years ago	Dec., 7 yrs. from now	4%	19
D	1,500	Jan., 2 years ago	Dec.,13 yrs. from now	10% every 5 years	19
E	1,000	Jan., 1 year ago	Dec., 9 yrs. from now	3%	20
F	1,200		Vacant (Projected Rent)		10

Read the lease notes below and complete the spreadsheet above, solving for the potential rental income (PRI) for *each year.* Remember that the analysis of this building is occurring in December of the current year.

Lease Notes:

Tenant A: Occupies 2,500 SF; the lease *expires December of this year;* current rent is $14 PSF. Annual escalations are irrelevant because the lease is expiring. Note: Current average rent in the building is $19 PSF and escalations average 3%. This is an old lease that is expiring at the end of this month. The tenant will either renew the lease at the market rate or be asked to leave. It is a reasonable assumption that a new lease starting next month will be at fair market value, the same average rent level and terms as the rest of the building.

Tenant B: Occupies 1,250 SF; lease expires in six years; current rent is $18 PSF; annual escalations equal 3%. In this case the rent increases three percent per year.

Tenant C: Occupies 1,250 SF; lease expires in seven years; current rent is $19 PSF; annual escalations equal 4%.

Tenant D: Occupies 1,500 SF; the lease started two years ago and expires in thirteen years; current rent is $19 PSF; escalations are 10% every five years. Because the lease started only two years ago, the first five-year increase will not occur for another three years.

Tenant E: Occupies 1,000 SF; lease expires in nine years; current rent is $20 PSF; annual escalations equal 3%.

Tenant F: Vacant space is 1,200 SF in the lower level; projected rent is $10 PSF and projected escalations are 3%. Assume this space will be rented in January.

Solution Step 1: Calculating the PRI					
Tenant	Current Year	Year 2	Year 3	Year 4	Year 5
A	$35,000	$47,500	$48,925	$50,393	$51,905
B	22,500	23,175	23,870	24,586	25,324
C	23,750	24,700	25,688	26,716	27,784
D	28,500	28,500	28,500	31,350	31,350
E	20,000	20,600	21,218	21,855	22,500
F	12,000	12,360	12,731	13,113	13,506
Total	$141,750	$156,835	$160,932	$168,013	$172,379

Tenant A: Because the lease expired in December of the current year, there is no rent escalation to calculate for the next year. Rather, a new lease starts in January (year 2), based on fair market value, with the average rent in the building at $19 PSF. The rent for the year 2000 is calculated at 2,500 SF × $19 PSF = $47,500.

The average rent escalations in the building are 3%, which will be used for this new lease.

Each year thereafter will be calculated as 1.03 times the prior years rent.
Year 3 Rent: $47,500 (prior years rent) × 1.03 = $48,925.
Year 4 Rent: $48,925 (prior years rent) × 1.03 = $50,393.
Year 5 Rent: $50,393 (prior years rent) × 1.03 = $51,905.

Tenant B: This lease started in four years ago and continues beyond the period of projections. Rent increases 3% per year.
Year 2 Rent: $22,500 (current year rent) × 1.03 = $23,175.
Year 3 Rent $23,175 (prior years rent) × 1.03 = $23,870.
Year 4 Rent: $23,870 × 1.03 = $24,586.
Year 5 Rent: $24,586 × 1.03 = $25,324.

Tenant C: This lease started in three years ago and continues beyond the period of projections. Rent increases 4% per year.
Year 2 Rent: $23,750 (prior years rent) × 1.04 = $24,700.
Year 3 Rent: $24,700 × 1.04 = $25,688.
Year 4 Rent: $25,688 × 1.04 = $26,716.
Year 5 Rent: $26,716 × 1.04 = $27,784.

Tenant D: This lease has a rent escalation that occurs every 5 years. The lease started 2 years ago and runs another 13 years. During the 5-year analysis, a rent increase is due in year 4. The current rent of $28,500 remains the same for years 2 and 3. The year 4 rent increases by 10%.
Year 3 Rent: $28,500 (prior years rent) × 1.10 = $31,350.
The next escalation in this lease occurs in year 10 of the lease, therefore the rent in year 5 is the same as the year 4 rent.

Tenant E: This lease started in last year and continues beyond the projection period. Rent increases 3% per year.
Year 2 Rent: $20,000 (prior years rent) × 1.03 = $20,600.
Year 3 Rent: $20,600 × 1.03 = $21,218.
Year 4 Rent: $21,218 × 1.03 = $21,855.
Year 5 Rent: $21,855 × 1.03 = $22,510.

Tenant F: This is vacant space. However, when we calculate Potential Rental Income (PRI), rent is projected for all space whether occupied or not. For purposes of this problem, the current rent was projected at $12,000, based on the average increase of 3% in the building. We are assuming that when the space is rented in the next year, it will be for 3% more.
Year 2 Rent: $12,000 (prior years projected rent) × 1.03 = $12,360.
Year 3 Rent: $12,360 (2000 rent) × 1.03 = $12,731.
Year 4 Rent: $12,731 × 1.03 = $13,113.
Year 5 Rent: $13,113 × 1.03 = $13,506.

The projected rents from each tenant for each year are added together to result in the Five-Year Projected Rental Incomes.

Small Office Building Problem, Part B

STEP 2

Calculate the cash flow before taxes (CFBT)

Once the potential rental income (PRI) for each year is known, that year's adjustments and expenses can be calculated to determine net operating income (NOI) and cash flow before taxes (CFBT). A spreadsheet is used again. Fill in the chart below. Then read through the table and analysis that follows this chart to check your answers.

	Current Year	Year 2	Year 3	Year 4	Year 5
Potential Rental Income (PRI)	$141,750	_____	_____	_____	_____
Vacancy Adjustment	_____	_____	_____	_____	_____
Other Income	_____	_____	_____	_____	_____
Gross Operating Income (GOI)	_____	_____	_____	_____	_____
Expenses:					
Taxes	_____	_____	_____	_____	_____
Repair and Maintenance	_____	_____	_____	_____	_____
All Other Expenses	_____	_____	_____	_____	_____
Total Expenses	_____	_____	_____	_____	_____
Net Operating Income (NOI)	_____	_____	_____	_____	_____

A recap of the problem's adjustments follows:

- An agreement allows a telephone company to have a relay antenna on the roof for a fee of $500 per month.

- The owner uses 7% as a vacancy adjustment, 5% for repair contingency *based on the Gross Operating Income (GOI)* and manages the building himself.

- Taxes are presently $50,000 per year but have just been reduced. The tax reductions are effective as follows: A reduction of $2,500 occurs in year 3, a further reduction of $2,500 occurs in year 4.

- All other operating expenses combine to $20,000 presently and are expected to increase at a rate of 3% per year.

Solution Step 2: Calculating the Cash Flow Before Taxes (CFBT)					
	Current Yr.	**Year 2**	**Year 3**	**Year 4**	**Year 5**
Potential Rental Income (PRI)	$141,750	$156,835	$160,932	$168,013	$172,379
Vacancy Adjustment	9,923	10,978	11,265	11,791	12,067
Other Income	6,000	6,000	6,000	6,000	6,000
Gross Operating Income (GOI)	137,827	151,857	155,667	162,252	166,312
Expenses:					
Taxes	50,000	50,000	47,500	45,000	45,000
Repair and Maintenance	6,891	7,593	7,783	8,113	8,316
All Other Expenses	20,000	20,600	21,218	21,885	22,510
Total Expenses	76,891	78,193	76,501	74,968	75,826
Net Operating Income (NOI)	60,936	73,664	79,166	87,284	90,486
Debt Service	45,642	45,642	45,642	45,642	45,642
Cash Flow Before Taxes	$15,294	$28,022	$33,524	$41,642	$44,844

Potential Rental Income (PRI): This was determined in Step 1 and was entered in line 1 of the spreadsheet above for each year.

Note that just like on the Annual Property Operating Data (APOD) checklist, each line is calculated for each year.

Vacancy Adjustment: The problem states that a 7% adjustment is made for vacancy. Multiplying the Potential Rental Income (POI) in line 1 for each year by .07 results in the dollar value of the Vacancy Adjustment.

Current Year:	$141,750	×	.07	=	$9,923.
Year 2:	$156,835	×	.07	=	$10,978.
Year 3:	$160,932	×	.07	=	$11,265.
Year 4:	$168,013	×	.07	=	$11,761.
Year 5:	$172,379	×	.07	=	$12,067.

The results are entered on line 2 of the chart.

Other Income: The problem has Other Income (not affected by vacancy), which is the antenna fee of $6,000 per year. This figure is inserted for each year in line 3, Other Income, on the chart.

Gross Operating Income, is the total, by year, of the previous entries. The Vacancy Adjustment is *subtracted* from the Potential Rental Income; the Other Income is *added* to that figure; the result is the Gross Operating Income (GOI).

As an example, this is the calculation for the Current Year:

Potential Rental Income	$141,750
Less Vacancy Adjustment	− 9,923
(Subtotal)	131,827
Plus Other Income	+ 6,000
Gross Operating Income	$137,827

Enter results for the other years in line 4.

Expenses

Taxes: Current taxes are $50,000 per year, which remains constant until year 3 when they will be reduced by $2,500 to $47,500. The tax rate is reduced again in year 4 by another $2,500 to $45,000, which remains the same for year 5. Results go on line 6.

Repairs and Maintenance: This contingency expense is being calculated in this problem as 5% of the Gross Operating Income (GOI), line 4. Enter results on line 7.

Just a reminder, some investors may take the percentage from the potential rental income (PRI) or the effective rental income (ERI) instead of the gross operating income (GOI). Some may use a fixed dollar amount. You must determine the basis of this calculation so that everyone is making the calculation in the same way.

For this problem, multiply the Gross Operating Income (GOI) for each year by 5%.

Current Year:	$137,827	×	.05	=	$6,891
Year 2:	$151,857	×	.05	=	$7,593
Year 3:	$155,667	×	.05	=	$7,783
Year 4:	$162,252	×	.05	=	$8,113
Year 5:	$166,312	×	.05	=	$8,316

Remaining Expenses: In this problem, all other expenses were lumped together as a single entry of $20,000 in the current year. It is projected that these expenses will increase by 3% each year.

To calculate the next year's expenses, multiply the current year by 1.03 and record in line 8.

Current Year:	$20,000				
Year 2:	$20,000	×	1.03	=	$20,600
Year 3:	$20,600	×	1.03	=	$21,218
Year 4:	$21,218	×	1.03	=	$21,885
Year 5:	$21,885	×	1.03	=	$22,510

Total Expenses: All expenses by year are now totaled in line 9.

Net Operating Income: For each year, subtracting the Total Expenses from the Gross Operating Income (GOI) results in the Net Operating Income (NOI). Results go on line 10.

Cash Flow Before Taxes (CFBT): This is determined by subtracting the Annual Debt Service, recorded on line 11, from the Net Operating Income (NOI).

Here is the calculation done for the first year.

Gross Operating Income	$137,827
Less Total Expenses	– 76,891
Net Operating Income	60,936
Less Annual Debt Service	–45,642
Cash Flow Before Taxes	$15,294

Reviewing the results of the Five-Year Forecast shows the significant upside potential of the building, as seen below.

	Current Year	Year 2	Year 3	Year 4	Year 5
Net Operating Income (NOI)	60,936	73,664	79,166	87,284	90,486
Cash Flow Before Taxes (CFBT)	15,294	28,022	33,524	41,642	44,844

We note the significant increase in the net operating income (NOI) and cash flow before taxes (CFBT) in year 2 as a result of bringing an old lease up to market value. There is another increase in revenue in year 4 when Tenant D's rent escalates by 10% and the Operating Expenses are reduced due to the tax reductions.

les³on

Returns on Investments

learning objectives

After completing this lesson, you will

■ understand the use of five-year projections,

■ be able to calculate different returns on investments, and

■ know how to determine market value.

■ Small Office Building Problem Part C

At the beginning of this analysis problem you calculated the present owner had a cash on cash return of 12.24 percent at this time. In the last "spreadsheet" lesson, the effects of certain upside events were reflected in the five-year projections; now calculate the cash on cash return for the next four years. Use the cash flow before taxes (CFBT) figures above in the formula below.

> **Cash Flow Before Taxes ÷ Initial Cash Investment = Cash on Cash Rate of Return**

■ Solution Small Office Building Problem Part C

The initial cash investment is the down payment, which was $125,000 when the current owner bought the building five years ago for $500,000. Utilizing the formula, the cash on cash returns for the projected five-year period are:

Current Year:	$15,294	÷	$125,000	=	.1224 or 12%
Year 2:	$28,022	÷	$125,000	=	.2242 or 22%
Year 3:	$33,524	÷	$125,000	=	.2682 or 27%
Year 4:	$41,642	÷	$125,000	=	.3331 or 33%
Year 5:	$44,844	÷	$125,000	=	.3588 or 36%

From the owner's position, the return on investment significantly increases from 12 percent to 36 percent over the examined period due to upside potential. We can also infer that for the first five years of ownership, the owner did not have a good return on the building and may actually have lost money. Now, however, it appears that the future return on investment is promising.

The owner's original question to the broker was: "What is my building worth?" Through this five-year analysis we have, so far, determined the owner's return on investment currently and projected into the future. However, will a new buyer be interested in the present owner's cash on cash return? Consider that the cash on cash return is based on the cash flow before taxes which is calculated from the present debt service expense and the down payment made by the owner when he bought the building.

Only if the potential owner was "taking over" the present mortgage and using the same down payment amount would the projected cash on cash return be a valid consideration to him or her.

This would also mean the building would be sold now for the same price that it was bought for—$500,000. It is rare in commercial transactions that a mortgage is assumed by a buyer. But, it is not unusual for a seller to offer to hold a first or second mortgage for a buyer.

■ Market Value

"What is my building worth?" To truly answer the question, the building must be looked at from the buyer's point of view: what will an investor pay for the building?

Investors will examine the property and create future projections just as we have done. As noted, they will generally not be concerned with current financing and cash flow before taxes (CFBT); their focus will be the net operating income (NOI). With that and a capitalization rate (CAP rate), market value can be determined.

The capitalization rate (CAP rate) is the desired profit percentage of an investor. For purposes of this problem, assume the market conditions have investors seeking a 10 percent to 12 percent return on their investments. If we combine the data collected from the seller with the current desired capitalization rates (CAP rates) of the buyers, we can reach some conclusions about the value of the property.

■ Small Office Building Problem Part D

Fill in the below chart with projected Market Value for each year at 10% and 12% CAP rates.

	Current Year	Year 2	Year 3	Year 4	Year 5
Net Operating Income (NOI)	$60,936	$73,664	$79,166	$87,284	$90,486
10% CAP rate	_____	_____	_____	_____	_____
12% CAP rate	_____	_____	_____	_____	_____

Remember, the formula for finding market value is as follows:

NOI ÷ CAP Rate = Market Value

Here is the sample calculation for the current year:

$60,936 (NOI) ÷ .10 (CAP Rate) = $609,360 (Market Value)

■ Solution—Small Office Building Problem Part D

	Current Year	Year 2	Year 3	Year 4	Year 5
Net Operating Income (NOI)	$60,936	$73,664	$79,166	$87,284	$90,486
10% CAP rate	$609,360	$736,640	$791,660	$872,840	$904,860
12% CAP rate	$507,800	$613,867	$659,717	$727,367	$754,050

■ The Original Problem

The current owner wants to know the value of the property. You are a commercial realtor who wants to list the building for sale. What do you advise the owner to expect as a sales price? Remember the building was bought for $500,000 five years ago, and it is now December of the current year.

This is a judgment call; there is no "correct" answer. However, consider the following points:

■ What the current owner paid is irrelevant to the next buyer.
■ Test the assumptions—projections—for "reality."
   ■ Because it is December, one might ignore the figures for the current year and begin with the year 2 figures. The major rent increase in year 2 is based upon replacing an old lease at market value. This is a valid assumption.

- The other major rent increase is scheduled for year 4 when Tenant D's 10 percent rent escalation occurs. Will this tenant still be in the building in three years?
- Expenses will decrease in year 3 forward as a result of tax reductions.
- How much of the upside potential will the buyer be willing to pay for?

What we have done with our property analysis is known as the "income approach" to valuation. This is typically the method used by bank appraisers to evaluate mortgage applications.

With this problem, if we assume the current year is over and start with year 2 figures as being valid, we might convince the buyers to use the year 3 projections as a basis for their offer.

Based on these numbers and the upside potential, especially with the future tax relief, you could justify telling the owner that his property could sell for $650,000. Perhaps a listing price of $700,000 to allow for negotiations might be appropriate. Because the seller paid $500,000, a sale at $650,000 would probably be agreeable to him.

■ Other Methods of Evaluation

However, we are only focusing here on the income methods of determining market value. Due consideration must be given to the two other methods of evaluation, the cost approach and comparable sales.

The "cost approach" looks at what is being paid for the building per square foot in comparison to what it would cost to construct the same building today. In this case, the cost per foot computes at (price divided by building size equals the cost per foot):

$$\$650,000 \div 8,700 \text{ SF} = \$74.71 \text{ PSF}$$

Depending on the market area, this could be a little high for a Class B building. Would someone buy a building if they could build it new for less construction cost? For an important location?

"Comparable sales" are required to complete the evaluation and confirm the projected value. Will the building appraise sufficiently to allow the desired financing?

These are all serious questions, requiring further consideration in answering your client's question, "What is my building worth?" You do, however, now have a detailed analysis and spreadsheets of realistic projections *based on the owner's numbers* to review with him.

 l e s s o n

The Buyer's Perspective

l e a r n i n g   o b j e c t i v e s

After completing this lesson, you will

- understand the buyer's perspective on investments, and
- know the key assumptions on which to negotiate.

Another important step is required to properly evaluate the value of the Office Building: The property must be also looked at from the buyer's perspective. Buyers will create their own pro forma, using the information provided by the seller, to determine what they consider to be the value of a building. The buyers may not agree with the assumptions or projections used by the owners in their operating statements.

■ Typical Operating Statement Challenges

Buyers may have many reasons to challenge operating statements of owners, but the following are most often encountered:

- Incorrectly stated facts
  - Lease details—expirations, escalations, renewals, options, or pass through expenses.
- Questionable assumptions
  - Vacancy projections
  - Repair & maintenance projections
- Business style
  - Management—off-site
  - Debt service—leveraging
- Replacement of tenants—projected rent amounts
  - Current market rent

Referring to the assumptions made in the last problem, the buyer might question several things.

For example, he could question the projected rent for the lower level space, which is indicated as immediately rentable at $12 PSF. How long has the space been vacant? Is it really rentable? For the current year, it is projected that the lower level space of 1,200 SF will be rented for $10 PSF—$12,000 annually. The buyer sees a "wet" basement that "will never be rented! Certainly not at $12 PSF." The buyer also could question any of the following:

Vacancy Adjustment Rate of 7%: The $12,000 projected rent from the basement is in fact 8.47% of the entire building's current potential rental income of $141,750. The present owner has used 7% for vacancy contingency. The buyer may consider a 10% vacancy contingency more realistic.

The Repairs and Maintenance Contingency Expense of 5%: This is a Class B building, and after the buyer's inspection and engineering report, it is felt a larger reserve is appropriate. The buyer uses 10% in his pro forma.

The Business Style: The current owner manages his own building. The buyer hires real estate brokers or property management companies to manage his properties and generally pays them 5 percent of the rent roll as a fee. A management expense is included in the buyer's pro forma.

The percentages mentioned in this section are not uncommon. Many clients target an investment acquisition at 75 percent of net operating income (NOI), considering 10 percent for vacancy, 10 percent for repair and maintenance, and 5 percent for management.

To illustrate this concept, let us compare the two perspectives, only changing the percentages used in the assumptions for vacancy, repair and maintenance, and adding management expense to the buyer's pro forma.

Investment Pro Forma: Seller's Perspective with Vacancy 7%, Repair & Maintenance 5%, No Management

	Current Year	Year 2	Year 3	Year 4	Year 5
Potential Rental Income (POI)	141,750	156,835	160,932	168,013	172,379
Vacancy Adjustment	9,923	10,978	11,265	11,791	12,067
Other Income	6,000	6,000	6,000	6,000	6,000
Gross Operating Income (GOI)	137,827	151,857	155,667	162,252	166,312
Expenses:					
Taxes	50,000	50,000	47,500	45,000	45,000
Repair and Maintenance	6,891	7,593	7,783	8,113	8,316
All Other Expenses	20,000	20,600	21,218	21,885	22,510
Total Expenses	76,891	78,193	76,501	74,968	75,826
Net Operating Income (NOI)	60,936	73,664	79,166	87,284	90,486

Investment Pro Forma: Buyer's Perspective with Vacancy 10%, Repair & Maintenance 10%, Management 5%

	Current Year	Year 2	Year 3	Year 4	Year 5
Potential Rental Income (POI)	141,750	156,835	160,932	168,013	172,379
Vacancy Adjustment	14,175	15,683	16,093	16,801	17,237
Other Income	6,000	6,000	6,000	6,000	6,000
Gross Operating Income (GOI)	133,575	147,152	150,839	157,212	161,142
Expenses:					
Taxes	50,000	50,000	47,500	45,000	45,000
Repair and Maintenance	13,357	14,715	15,083	15,721	16,114
Management	6,679	7,358	7,542	7,861	8,057
All Other Expenses	20,000	20,600	21,218	21,885	22,510
Total Expenses	90,036	92,673	91,343	90,436	91,681
Net Operating Income (NOI)	43,539	54,479	59,496	66,776	69,461

■ Quite a difference!

Different perspectives make quite a difference in the buyer's and seller's pro formas. If we now use the same formulas for determining market value based on net operating income (NOI) and capitalization rate (CAP rate), we see the full impact of the different perspectives.

Seller's Perspective of Market Value					
	Current Year	Year 2	Year 3	Year 4	Year 5
10% CAP	$609,360	$736,640	$791,660	$872,840	$904,860
12% CAP	$507,800	$613,867	$659,717	$727,367	$754,050

Buyer's Perspective of Market Value					
	Current Year	Year 2	Year 3	Year 4	Year 5
10% CAP	$435,000	$545,000	$595,000	$668,000	$695,000
12% CAP	$363,000	$454,000	$496,000	$556,000	$579,000

As you can see, there is quite a difference in the perceived market values between the property owner and the potential buyer. In our problem, none of the "facts" changed; both analyses used the same rent-roll information and expenses. What did change were the assumptions: vacancy contingency rate, repair and maintenance percentage, and business style regarding management.

■ Evaluating Assumptions

Consider the following questions when evaluating the assumptions that caused the discrepancies between the two perspectives.

Vacancy Adjustment Rate

- What is the reality?
- How strong is the local market?
- What are the vacancy rates of comparable buildings in the area?
- Is the desired rent competitive?

Repair and Maintenance Percentage

- What is realistic?
- What is the condition and age of the building?
- What does the engineer's report say?
- What are the landlord's responsibilities versus the tenants' obligations in the leases?

Management Expenses

■ Is it a fair comparison when one party does their own management and the other uses off-site management?

■ Commercial Brokerage Responsibilities

In order to do our job properly, we must look at the property from both perspectives (the owner's and potential buyer's), validate the facts, and evaluate the assumptions.

Negotiate the assumptions first. If both sides can agree on these variables and all the other figures are verified, a fair price range can be developed. Within this price range, a "deal" can be made that is fair to both sides. This is how we, commercial brokers, do our job.

The problem looked at throughout this Chapter was a typical one found in the commercial and investment real estate brokerage business. This exercise was designed to show you how some buyers think, how some investors evaluate for negotiating purposes, and to show you there are no absolutes—just guidelines created by formulas, estimates and projections.

The commercial buyer—a user is driven by the need to expand or reduce their business operation. The investment buyer is driven by profit—current income from the property and future upside potential. Both commercial and investment customers will pay for the real estate situation that works for them.

In commercial and investment real estate, we develop relationships with our customers for life. As time goes on, their business needs and requirements change, their leases end, or they are ready for another investment. We service our clients over and over again. It is extremely important in all our transactions that everyone is satisfied with the deal, that the buyers and sellers feel they got a fair deal.

■ Chapter 7 Review Questions

1. As the CAP rate goes up, the value
   a. increases.
   b. decreases.
   c. is not affected.
   d. remains the same.

2. The cash on cash return is most important to the
   a. seller.
   b. buyer.
   c. bank.
   d. broker.

3. When buying a property, which method of market valuation should be used?
   a. Income approach
   b. Comparable sales
   c. Cost approach
   d. All of the above

4. What might a buyer question in his or her pro forma?
   a. Vacancy projections
   b. Contingent repair expenses
   c. Lease details
   d. All of the above

5. What expense item is usually based on a percentage?
   a. Taxes
   b. CAM charges
   c. Management fees
   d. Accounting fees

6. Repair and maintenance contingency expense may be determined by
   a. calculating a percentage of the Gross Operating Income.
   b. calculating a percentage of the Potential Rental Income.
   c. using a specific dollar amount.
   d. All of the above.

7. In order to sell investment properties, one should first negotiate the
   a. assumptions.
   b. price.
   c. terms.
   d. CAP rate.

8. A spreadsheet shows
   a. future market value.
   b. comparable sales data.
   c. projected income and expenses.
   d. all of the above.

9. Leveraging has what effect on an investment?
   a. Always increases the rate of return
   b. Always decreases the rate of return
   c. Reduces the initial investment
   d. Helps sell the property

10. What is the most important figure to an investment buyer?
    a. CAP rate
    b. cash on cash return
    c. CFBT
    d. NOI

Chapter 1 Review Questions

1. *c.* A golf course is commercially developed land.
2. *d.* Almost all commercial properties can be investments.
3. *b.* The developer builds for the tenant, according to the tenant's specifications.
4. *c.* Property is developed, tenanted, and usually immediately sold.
5. *b.* The "bottom line" is the return on the investment.
6. *a.* The decision is financial, based on the return on the investment in dollars.

Chapter 2 Review Questions

1. *d.* Taxpayer is a common term for small multiuse buildings.
2. *a.* The ground floor area is known as the footprint.
3. *c.* This is the basic investment concept; gross operating income less owner's operative expenses equals net operating income.
4. *b.* Required IRS depreciation of commercial buildings is over 39 years.
5. *d.* Only buildings depreciate, land does not.
6. *d.* These are all good reasons for buying instead of leasing.
7. *b.* Mortgage expense is not included in operating expenses. Not every property will be financed; some investors buy "all cash."
8. *a.* Potential rental income (PRI) includes all rentable space occupied or not.
9. *b.* Debt service is the total annual expense of mortgage payments (principal and interest).
10. *d.* Often a user will become an investor too.

Chapter 3 Review Questions

1. *c.* Large stores, such as supermarkets, are found in shopping centers.
2. *b.* Potential rental income (PRI) is adjusted for vacancy contingency.
3. *d.* How long a space may be unoccupied is a consideration in calculating vacancy.
4. *d.* Gross operating income (GOI) results after adjustments to the rent roll.
5. *d.* Credit losses result from lost rent by existing tenants.
6. *b.* Vacancy percentage is determined by a "reality check" of the property and area.
7. *d.* Operating expenses include all property expenses paid by the owner.
8. *c.* Roof repair would be a contingency expense under "Repair & Maintenance."
9. *d.* Each choice is a regular and routine expense of the property.
10. *a.* "Repair & Maintenance" can be a percentage of Potential Rental Income (PRI) or Gross Operating Income (GOI) or a fixed amount of money.

Chapter 4 Review Questions

1. *a.* Banks look at appraised values on any kind of real estate in considering mortgages.
2. *c.* Net operating income (NOI) divided by price (value) equals the capitalization rate (CAP rate) return on the investment.

3. *d.* Timing affects what a client will accept and what a customer will pay.
4. *c.* A Triple Net Lease (NNN) requires the tenant to pay all expenses.
5. *b.* Floor area ratio (FAR) determines how large a building may be on a given site.
6. *c.* Highest and best use attempts to maximize the potential profit from a property.
7. *c.* Improvements belong to the land owner.
8. *d.* The capitalization rate (CAP rate) reflects investors desired rates of return.
9. *a.* Value is equal to the net operating income (NOI) divided by the capitalization rate (CAP rate).
10. *b.* $90,000 (NOI) ÷ .09 (9% CAP rate) equals $1,000,000 Market Value.

Chapter 5 Review Questions

1. *c.* The advertising done by an anchor store lures people to a shopping center.
2. *b.* Common area maintenance (CAM) includes shared services for all the tenants.
3. *a.* A tax escalation clause requires tenants to pay their proportionate share of increases.
4. *d.* Gross leasable area (GLA) is all possible rental space on the property.
5. *c.* Income (affected by vacancy) generally includes common area maintenance (CAM) and tax escalation income.
6. *d.* Percentages are always used to calculate vacancy and management expense and, generally, are used to calculate repair and maintenance.
7. *b.* Gross operating income (GOI) minus total operating expenses (TOE) equals net operating income (NOI).
8. *d.* "Other Income" sources are not affected by tenants.
9. *b.* On an Annual Property Data (APOD) form all figures must be converted to annual income or expense.
10. *a.* An Annual Property Data (APOD) form is a tool to gather the data necessary for financial analysis.

Chapter 6 Review Questions

1. *b.* Leveraging is the use of borrowed funds to finance a portion of the cost of an investment.
2. *b.* Cash on cash return equals cash flow before taxes (CFBT) divided by the initial investment, i.e., the down payment.
3. *c.* Cash flow before taxes (CFBT) equals net operating income (NOI) minus annual debt service.
4. *d.* Internal rate of return (IRR) considers the entire holding period of an investment.
5. *a.* The capitalization rate (CAP rate) is the desired profit percentage of investors.
6. *d.* Net operating income (NOI) minus annual debt service equals cash flow before taxes (CFBT).
7. *d.* With favorable mortgage terms and interest rates, leveraging increases the cash on cash return.
8. *b.* Here the capitalization rate (CAP rate) formula is used to determine the return on investment (ROI) with net operating income (NOI) divided by Value equaling CAP (ROI): $67,500 (NOI) ÷ $450,000 (Value) = .15 or 15% return on investment (ROI).

9. *b.* To calculate cash on cash return, one must first calculate cash flow before taxes (CFBT). Net operating income (NOI) minus annual debt service equals cash flow before taxes (CFBT).
$67,500 (NOI) – $38,934 (debt service) = $28,566 (CFBT)
CFBT divided by the initial investment = cash on cash return
$28,566 (CFBT) ÷ $100,000 (Initial Investment) = .2857 or 29% Cash on Cash Return

10. *b.* $28,566 (CFBT) ÷ $200,000 (Initial Investment) = .1428 or 14% Cash on Cash Return. Because calculators automatically round off, it is suggested you calculate using four digits.

Chapter 7 Review Questions

1. *b.* The higher the capitalization rate (CAP rate) desired, the less an investor will pay for a property.
2. *a.* The cash on cash return reflects the owner (seller's) return based on down payment and financing.
3. *d.* Because market value can be determined by three different methods, it is best to consider all three when pricing a property.
4. *d.* A buyer will question all assumptions and verify all information.
5. *c.* Management fees are typically a percentage of the rent roll.
6. *d.* Repair and maintenance expenses may be a calculated as a percentage of gross operating income (GOI) or potential rental income (PRI) or a specific dollar amount.
7. *a.* If buyer and seller can agree on the assumptions made for percentage adjustments for vacancy, repair and management, the price will be narrowed down for final negotiations.
8. *c.* Projections of income, expense, and net operating income (NOI) are used to calculate current and future market value.
9. *c.* Leveraging implies a mortgage in lieu of an all cash purchase, reducing the amount of the initial investment to a down payment.
10. *d.* The net operating income (NOI) used in conjunction with the investor's desired capitalization rate (CAP rate) will determine the buyer's value of the property.

abatement A reduction or decrease; usually applies to the forgiveness of rent or a decrease of assessed valuation of ad valorem taxes after the assessment and levy.

above building standard Specialized design and engineering services and all construction necessary to personalize tenant space.

absorbed space Net change in leased space between two dates.

absorption The rate at which land or buildings will be sold or leased in the marketplace during a predetermined period of time, usually a month or a year. Also called "Market Absorption."

absorption period The number of months required to convert vacant space into leased space assuming no new delivered space. Computed by dividing the average monthly absorbed space during a recent period into the current vacant space.

ad valorem (According to value) Used in reference to general property tax, which is usually based on the official valuation of property.

add-on factor Considered a loss factor, the percentage of gross rentable square footage that is lost to the tenant's physical occupancy.

adequate rate covenant An agreement often required in revenue bond-financed projects; guarantees the operator will charge adequate rates to produce revenue necessary to cover principal and interest payments.

alienation clause A type of acceleration clause where a debt becomes due in its entirety upon the transfer of ownership of a secured property. *See also* "Due on Sales Clause" and "Acceleration Clause."

allowance over building shell One of three arrangements often used for financing tenant improvements (finishing out office space to accommodate a tenant such as walls, doors, carpeting, etc.). Often used in a yet-to-be-built building, this arrangement caps the landlord's expenditure at a fixed dollar amount over the negotiated price of the base building shell. This arrangement is most successful when both parties agree on a detailed definition of what construction is included and at what price. Tenants may ask for a contingency in the event that the actual build-out costs are less than the allowance, requiring the landlord to return the savings in the form of rent abatement or other concession.

AM Accredited Member (designation offered by the American Society of Appraisers).

annual percentage rate (APR) APR reflects the cost of a loan on a yearly basis. It may be higher than the note rate because it includes interest, loan origination fees, loan discount points, and other credit costs paid to the lender.

anticipatory breach Occurs when one party to a contract, prior to time of performance, informs the other of his or her intent not to perform. Example The buyer informs the seller before the closing date of his or her intent not to buy.

appraisal The estimation and opinion of value placed upon a piece of land based upon a factual analysis by a qualified professional; the process of estimation and the report itself.

appreciation An increase in the value of property caused by an improvement of the elimination of negative factors.

ASA Accredited Senior Appraiser (designation offered by the American Society of Appraisers).

"as is" condition Premises accepted by a buyer or tenant in the condition existing at the time of sale or lease, including all physical defects.

assessment (1) An estimate of property value for the purpose of imposing taxes. (2) A fee imposed on property, usually to pay for public improvements such as streets and sewers.

asset-based lender A lender who loans money based primarily on the values of an asset—accounts receivable, inventory, a piece of equipment, real estate—rather than on the financial strength of the business, which is the primary criterion for banks.

assignment A transfer between parties of title to any property, real or personal, or of any rights or estates in the property. Common assignments include leases, mortgages, and deeds of trust.

attachment Legal procedure to aid in the collection of a debt. Usually the court issues a writ to seize the property of a debtor and holds it pending the outcome of a lawsuit, keeping the property available for sale to pay any money judgment entered in such lawsuit.

attorn To turn over or transfer to another money or goods. To agree to recognize a new owner of a property and to pay him rent. *See also* "Letter of Attornment."

balloon payment A large payment due on a loan. Generally a balloon payment is required when regular monthly or quarterly payments have not covered both the increase due and the principal of the loan.

bankrupt The condition when one is found to be unable to repay one's debts by a court having the proper jurisdiction. The bankruptcy may be one of two types: one that is petitioned by the debtor (voluntary) or petitioned by the creditors (involuntary).

bankruptcy Proceedings under federal statutes to relieve a debtor who has been declared bankrupt from insurmountable debt. After addressing certain priorities and exemptions, the bankrupt's property and other assets are distributed by the court to creditors as full satisfaction for the debt. *See also* "Chapter 11."

base rent A set amount used as a minimum rent in a lease that also employs a percentage or other allocation for additional rent.

base year The year upon which a direct expense escalation of rent is based. *See also* "Escalation Clause."

below-grade Any facility or part of a facility located underground or below the surface grade.

breach of warranty The failure of the seller of real property to pass title as either expressed or implied by law in the conveyance document.

buffer A strip of land established as a transition between distinct land uses. May contain natural or planted shrubs, walls or fencing, singly or in combination.

building classifications Class "A"—Building has excellent location and access to attract the highest quality tenants. Building must be of superior construction and finish, relatively new or competitive with new buildings, and providing professional on-site management. Class "B" —Building with good location, management, construction land tenancy. Can complete at low end of Class A. Class "C"—Generally an older building with growing functional land/or economic obsolescence. Class "D"—An older building in need of extensive renovation as a result of functional obsolescence or deterioration.

building code A set of laws, usually enacted by city ordinance or other local jurisdiction, regulating the design, materials and construction of buildings.

building standard A list of construction materials and finishes used in building out office space for a tenant that the landlord contributes as part of the tenant improvements. Examples of standard building items are doors, partitions, lights, floor covering, telephone outlets, etc. May also specify the quantity and quality of the materials to be used and often carries a dollar value. *See also* "Workletter."

building standard plus allowance One of three arrangements often used for financing tenant improvements (finishing out office space to accommodate a tenant such as walls, doors, carpeting, etc.) Under this arrangement, the land lists in detail all materials and costs to make the premises suitable for occupancy and provides a negotiated allowance for the tenant to customize or upgrade materials. *See also* "Workletter."

buildout The cost of configuring and finishing new or relet space in accordance with a tenant's specifications.

build to suit A method of leasing property whereby the landlord builds a new building in accordance with a tenant's specifications.

bullet loan Also known as a Construction Loan, any of a variety of short-term (generally five to seven years) financings provided by a lender to a developer to cover the costs of construction and lease-up of a new building with the expectation that it would be replaced by long-tern (or "permanent") financing provided by an institutional investor once most of risk involved in construction and lease-up has been overcome, resulting in an income-producing property.

CAM Certified Asset Manager

C.A.M. Common Area Maintenance

capitalization A process of determining the value of real property in which project income is divided by a predetermined annual rate (capitalization rate). For example, a building with annual project income of $100,000 is worth $1,000,000 at a 10 percent capitalization rate ($100,000/10% = $1,000,000). *See also* "Capitalization Rate."

capitalization rate The rate that is considered a reasonable return on investment (on the basis of both the investor's alternative investment possibilities and the risk of the investment.) Used to determine and value real property through the capitalization process. Also called, "free and clear return." *See also* "Capitalization."

carrying charges Various costs that are incidental to property ownership (e.g., taxes, insurance costs, and maintenance expenses).

CCIM Certified Commercial Investment Member

certificate of occupancy A certificate issued by a local government building department or agency stating that a building is in a condition suitable for occupancy. Sometimes also called a "C of O" or a Non-Residential Use and Occupancy Permit (NON RUP).

chapter 11 A section of the Federal Bankruptcy Code dealing with business reorganizations. A separate section, referred to as Chapter 7, deals with business liquidations.

clear-span facility A parking structure with vertical columns on the outside edges of the structure and a clear span between columns, making it unnecessary for vehicles to maneuver between columns.

common area The total area within the shopping center that is not designed for rental to tenants but that is available for common use by all tenants or groups of tenants, their invitees, and adjacent stores. Parking and its appurtenances, malls, sidewalks, landscaped areas, public toilets, truck and service facilities, and the like are included in the common area.

common area charges Include income collected from tenants for operating and maintaining items pertaining to common areas. Shopping center leases usually contain a clause requiring the tenant to pay its share of operation and maintenance on common areas and defining the basis on which charges are made and the type of cost items allocable to maintenance of the common area. Of the ways to prorate the charges among tenants, the most common are (1) a prorated charge based on a tenant's leased area as a portion of the total leased area of the center or the linear exposure in store frontage, (2) a fixed charge for a stated period, and (3) a variable charge based on a percentage of sales. Some centers include a cost-of-living increase in the common area charges.

comparables Recorded sales of properties similar in size, use, construction quality, age, and often located within the same submarket used as comparisons to determine the fair market value of another particular property.

competitive space Space in office buildings that contain or are intended to contain more than one occupant. In addition to the multiple tenant criterion, typical characteristics of Competitive Space include tenants generally have short-term leases (10 years or less) and the interior of the building is not designed with one organization in mind but rather to accommodate the widest variety of tenants.

concessions Cash expended by the landlord in the form of rent abatement, build-out allowance, or other payments to induce the tenant to sign a lease.

condemnation The process by which private property is taken by a governmental agency for public use without the consent of the owner, but only upon payment of just compensation. *See also* "Eminent Domain."

construction management Construction supervision by a qualified manager.

consumer price index (CPI) A federal government index that measures the change in the cost of a variety of goods and services. Used in loans, purchase agreements and leases as a measure by which to adjust future payments to reflect inflation. Also called "Cost-of-Living Index."

contiguous space Adjoining office space.

contract documents The design plans and specifications for construction of a facility. Working drawings that detail for the contractor the exact manner in which a project should be built. *See also* "Specifications," "Working Drawings."

contract rent Rent paid under a lease. The actual rent as opposed to the market rental value of the property.

conveyance Most commonly refers to the transfer of title to land between parties. The term may also include most of the instruments by which an interest in real estate is created, mortgaged, or assigned.

core factor The percentage of common areas in a building (rest rooms, hallways) that, when added to the net usable square footage, equals the net rentable square footage. May be computed for a building or floor of a building. A "Loss Factor" or "Load Factor" is calculated by dividing the rentable square footage by the usable square footage. *See also* "Design Efficiency."

cost approach A method of appraising real property whereby the replacement cost of a structure is calculated using current costs of construction.

covenant A private, legal restriction on the use of land, recorded in the land records.

covenant of quiet enjoyment Usually inserted in leases or conveyances whereby landlord or grantor promises that the tenant or grantee shall enjoy possession of the premises in peace and quiet without disturbance.

CPM Certified Property Manager

CRE Counselor of Real Estate

cumulative discount rate A discount factor applied to the rental rate that takes into effect all landlord lease concessions expressed as a percentage of base rent.

dedicate Transfer of property from private to public ownership.

deed Generally, a conveyancing instrument given by the seller to pass fee title to property upon sale.

deed in lieu of foreclosure A deed given by an owner/borrower to a lender to prevent the lender from bringing foreclosure proceedings.

deed of trust An instrument securing a loan that is used in many states in place of a mortgage. Property that is transferred to a trustee by the borrower (trustor), in favor of the lender (beneficiary), and reconveyed to the borrower upon payment in full.

default The general failure to perform a promised task or to pay an obligation when due. Some specific examples are (1) Failure to make a payment of principal or interest or other type of financial obligation when due. (2) The breach of failure to perform any of the terms of a note or the convenants of a mortgage or deed of trust.

deficiency judgment Commonly, the amount for which the borrower is personally liable on a note and mortgage if the foreclosure sale does not bring enough to cover the amount owed. Actually, the judgment is for the total amount of the obligation and not for the deficiency. Any recoveries from a foreclosure sale are deducted from the judgment.

delivered buildings Buildings that have complete construction and are ready for tenant build-out. May or may not yet have a Certificate of Occupancy.

demising walls The boundaries that separate a tenant's space from another tenant's space and from a public corridor.

density Number of dwelling units divided by the gross acreage being developed.

design/build A system in which a single entity is responsible for both the design and construction of a facility, often involving the fast-track method of construction; also referred to as "design/construct."

depreciation (1) Decrease in the usefulness, and therefore value, of real property improvements or other assets caused by deterioration or obso-

lescence. (2) A loss in value as an accounting procedure to use as a deduction for income tax purposes.

distraint The act of taking (legally or illegally) personal property and retaining control until the property owner performs an obligation. Commonly, a landlord takes possession of personal property of a tenant in default until the default is satisfied.

distress sale The sale of property under less than favorable conditions. Usually, the seller is experiencing financial difficulties and is under extreme pressure to sell.

earnest money The monetary advance by a purchaser of part of the purchase price as evidence of good faith. The earnest money is used to bind the parties to the contract of sale.

easement A right to use the property of another created by grant, reservation, agreement, prescription or necessary implication. It is either for the right to cross A to get to B, or "in gross," such as a public utility easement.

economic feasibility A project's feasibility in terms of costs and revenue, with excess revenue establishing the degree of feasibility.

economic rent Calculations or analysis to determine market rental value of a property at any given time, even though the actual rent may be different.

effective rent The rental rate actually achieved by the landlord after deducting the value of concessions from the base rental rate paid by a tenant, usually expressed as an average rate over the term of the lease.

efficiency factor The number resulting from dividing the Usable Area by the Gross Building Area in an office building, providing a benchmark measurement for that building's use as an office building.

eminent domain A right of the government to acquire private property for public use by condemnation, in return for just compensation. *See also* "Condemnation."

encroachment Generally, a structure which extends impermissibly over a property line, easement boundary or building setback line.

encumbrance Any right to, or interest in, real property that may exist in one other than the owner, but which will not prevent the transfer of fee title. A claim, lien, charge or liability attached to and binding real property.

environmental impact report A report generally prepared by an independent company detailing the probable environmental effect of a development of the surrounding area.

equity The value of one's interest in a property, consisting of its fair market value less any outstanding debt or other encumbrances.

equity kicker Also called a participation loan. Under this kind of loan—often used by non-bank lenders with start-up businesses—the lender gets not only interest payments and principal repaid, but the right to buy equity (part ownership in the company) as well. Equity participation is generally required for riskier deals or in return for lower rates.

equity participation The participation by a lender in the equity ownership of a project as one of the conditions for granting a loan. Used by financial institutions to partially offset the effects of inflation. Also called "Equity Kicker."

equity of redemption Not the same as the redemption period after a foreclosure sale, which is a right established by payment of the principal, interest, and costs due.

escalation clause A clause in a lease providing for increased rent at a future time. May be accompanied by several means such as (1) Fixed increase—A provision that calls for a definite, periodic rental increase; (2) Cost of living—A clause that ties the rent to a government cost of living index, with periodic adjustments as the index changes; or (3) Direct expense—Rent adjustments based on changes in expenses paid by the landlord, such as tax increases, increased maintenance costs, etc.

escrow agreement A written agreement usually made between a buyer, seller and escrow agent. The escrow agreement sets forth the basic obligations of the parties, describes the objects deposited in escrow, and instructs the escrow agent concerning the disposition of the objects deposited.

estoppel certificate A statement concerning the status of an agreement and the performance of obligations under the agreement relied upon by a third party, including a prospective lender or purchaser. In the context of a lease, a statement by a tenant identifying that the lease is in effect and certifying that no rent has been prepaid and that there are no known outstanding defaults by the landlord (except those specified).

exclusive listing A written agreement between a real estate broker and a building owner in which the owner promises to pay a fee or commission to the broker if specified real property is sold or leased during a stated period. The broker may or may not be the cause of the sale or lease.

expense stop Provision in a lease establishing the maximum level of operating expense(s) to be paid by the landlord. Expenses beyond this level are to be reimbursed by the tenant. May be applied to specific expenses only (e.g., property taxes or insurance).

face rental rate The "asking" or nominal rental rate published by the landlord.

fair market value A term usually found in appraisals that attempts to determine the cash price that would likely be negotiated between a willing seller and a willing buyer in a reasonable amount of time. For a sale to be considered a reflection of "Fair Market Value," it must meet all the conditions of a fair sale whereby (1) both buyer and seller act prudently, knowledgeably and under no necessity to buy or sell, i.e., other than in a forced or liquidation sale; (2) the property must be offered on the open market for a reasonable amount of time, taking into consideration the property type and local market; and (3) payment is made in cash or terms equivalent to cash. When a sale is unlikely, i.e., when it is unlikely to be completed within 12 months, the appraiser must discount all cash flows generated by the property to ascertain the estimate of Fair Value.

feasibility study An analysis of needs, costs of recommended improvements, and anticipated revenue and costs; establishes the basis for the construction of an individual improvement or a complete system.

fee simple An estate of real property that the owner has unrestricted powers to dispose of and which can be left by will or inherited. Commonly used as a synonym for ownership.

finance charge The cost of credit as a dollar amount. It includes any charges payable by the borrower as a condition of the loan. The finance charge includes the total amount of interest, points, loan fees and other credit charges paid for the term of the loan.

FIRREA The Financial Institutions Reform Recovery and Enforcement Act of 1989. Created the Resolution Trust Corporation (RTC) and placed new restrictions on savings and loans regarding real estate investment.

first mortgage A mortgage creating a lien against a property that has priority over all other voluntary liens that exist against the property. Foreclosure of a first mortgage lien will generally extinguish or cut off any second mortgage lien or other subordinate lien.

first refusal right A clause occasionally inserted in a lease that gives a tenant the first opportunity to buy a property if the owner decides to sell. The owner must have a legitimate offer that the tenant can match or refuse.

fixed costs Costs, such as rent, which do not fluctuate in proportion to the level of sales or productions.

flex space A one- or two-story building with little or no common areas, high ceilings, load-bearing floors and loading dock facilities. Usually configured to allow a small amount of office space in combination with light assembly or warehouse/distribution uses.

floor/area ratio (FAR) The ratio of the bulk area of a building to the land on which it is situated. Calculated by dividing the total square footage of land area.

floodplain Land adjoining a river that would flood if the river overflows its banks.

force majeure A force that cannot be controlled or resisted. In other words, something beyond the control of the parties involved. Includes acts of God (e.g., flood, tornadoes, etc.) and acts of man (e.g., riots, strikes, arson, etc.).

foreclosure A proceeding, in or out of court, designed to extinguish all rights, title, and interest of the owner(s) of property in order to sell the property to satisfy a lien against it.

full recourse A borrowing with an unconditional guaranty. Should the borrower become delinquent under a full recourse loan, he or she must accept full responsibility for the loan.

full service rent A rental rate that includes operating expenses and real estate taxes for the first year. The tenant is generally still responsible for any increases in operating expenses over the base year amount. *See also* "Pass Throughs."

functional design Design of a structure or facility that increases its overall efficiency and provides maximum user acceptance; a parking concept plan showing traffic flow, stall geometry, and other features that determine the interior design of parking facilities.

future proposed space Commercial space in proposed development projects, which either have not stared construction, or set a construction start date. Future proposed projects include all those waiting for a lead tenant, financing, zoning, approvals, or any other event necessary to begin construction. Also may refer to the future phases of a multi-phase project that have not yet been built.

general contractor The party that contracts for the construction of an entire building or project, rather than a portion of the work. The general contractor hires subcontractors (e.g., plumbing contractors, electrical contractors, etc.), coordinates all work, and is responsible for payment to the subcontractors.

general partner A member of a partnership who has authority to bind the partnership. A general partner also shares in the profits and losses of the partnership. *See also* "Limited Partnership."

graduated lease A lease, generally long term in nature, with varied rental payments and usually based on periodic appraisal or simply the passage of time.

grant To transfer an interest in real property; either the fee or a lesser interest, such as an easement.

grantee One to whom a grant of property or property rights is made; generally, the buyer.

grantor One who grants property or property rights; generally, the seller.

gross absorption Absorption is a measure of the amount of office space leased over a period of time. Gross absorption is a measure of the total square feet leased over a period of time with no consideration for office space vacated in the same area during the same period. *See also* "Net Absorption."

gross building area The total floor area in an office building measured in square feet or square meters that is associated with the building's use as office building. The area extends to the outer surface of exterior walls and windows and includes office area, retail area, and other rentable areas such as vending machine space and storage area, but excludes parking and roof space.

gross lease A lease that provides that the landlord shall pay all expenses of the leased property, such as taxes, insurance, maintenance, utilities, etc.

ground lease A lease covering the use of land only, with the lease sometimes secured by improvements installed by the tenant. Also called a Land Lease.

ground rent Rent paid for vacant unimproved property. If the property is improved, ground rent is that portion of the total earnings attributable to the land only.

guarantor One who makes a guaranty. *See also* "Guaranty."

guaranty Agreement whereby the guarantor agrees to pay the debt or perform the obligation of another who fails to do so. Differs from a surety agreement in that there must be a failure to pay or perform before the guaranty can be in effect.

hard dollars The actual cash proceeds from a loan that is given to the seller. *See also "Soft Dollars."*

highest and best use The reasonably probable and legal use of vacant land or an improved property, which is physically possible, appropriately supported, financially feasible, and that results in the highest value. The four criteria the highest and best use must meet are: legal permissibility, physical possibility, financial feasibility, and maximum profitability.

high rise A building higher than 25 stories above ground level.

hold over tenant A tenant who retains possession after the expiration of a lease.

HVAC The acronym for Heating, Ventilating, and Air-Conditioning. Refers to the equipment used to heat and cool a building.

improved value An appraisal term that encompasses the total value of land and improvements rather than the separate values of each.

improvements Generally, the term refers to buildings, but may include any permanent structure or other development, such as a street, utilities, etc.

indirect costs Development costs other than direct material or direct labor costs, including administrative and office expenses, financing costs, and property taxes.

inventory When referring to a market of office or industrial space, the total amount of rentable square feet of existing and delivered space in a given category; for example, prime office space. Inventory refers to all space within a certain proscribed market without regard to its availability or condition, and can include both office and flax and warehouse space.

involuntary conveyance An involuntary transfer of real property without the consent of the owner, such as by a divorce decree, condemnation, etc.

judgment The decision of a court of law. Money judgments, when recorded, become a lien on real property of the defendant.

judgment lien A lien placed against the property of a judgment debtor. An involuntary lien.

judgment mortgage A mortgage creating a lien that is inferior or subordinate to a prior lien.

Foreclosure of a junior mortgage will not extinguish any lien that is superior to it. *See also "First Mortgage;" "Second Mortgage."*

just compensation In a condemnation proceeding, the term refers to the amount paid to the property owner. The theory is that in order to be "just," the property owner should be no richer or poorer than before the taking.

land contract An installment contract for the sale of land whereby the seller has legal title until paid in full. They buyer has equitable title during the contract term.

landlord's lien Several types of landlord's liens are created by contract or by statute. Some examples are 1) a contractual landlord's lien; 2) statutory landlord's lien; and 3) landlord's remedy of distress (or right of distraint), which is not truly a lien but has a similar effect.

landlord's warrant A warrant enabling a landlord to levy upon a tenant's personal property (e.g., furniture, etc.) and to sell this property at a public sale to collect delinquent rent.

land, tenements and hereditaments Originally used to describe freehold estates only. The terms have come to mean the most technical and all-inclusive description of real estate.

lease An agreement whereby the owner of real property (i.e., landlord) gives the right of possession to another (i.e., tenant) for a specific period of time (i.e., term) and for a specific consideration (i.e., rent).

lease commencement date The date on which beneficial occupancy commences and the legal terms of the lease go into effect.

leasehold improvements Improvements made to lease premises by a tenant. *See also "Tenant Improvements," "Workletter."*

legal description A method of geographically identifying a parcel of land that is acceptable in a court of law.

legal owner The term is used to distinguish the legal owner from the equitable owner and not as opposed to an illegal owner. The legal owner has title to the property, although the title may actually carry no rights to the property other than to act as a lien.

legal title Usually the title without the ownership rights, such as the title placed in a trustee under a deed of trust, or the title in a vendor under a land contract.

letter of credit An engagement, pledge, or commitment by a bank or person, made at the request of the customer, stating that the issuer will honor drafts or other demands for payment upon full compliance with the conditions specified in the letter of credit.

letter of attornment A letter from a grantor to a tenant, stating that a property has been sold, and directing rent to be paid to the grantee (i.e., the new owner). *See also* "Attorn."

letter of intent A formal method through which a prospective developer, buyer, or tenant expresses his/her interest in property. Depending on the language, a legal obligation may be created.

lien An encumbrance against property for money, either voluntary or involuntary. All liens are encumbrances, but all encumbrances are not liens.

lienholder A mortgagee or other creditor who has a lien against the property of another.

lien waiver (waiver of liens) Generally a waiver of mechanic's lien rights signed by a general contractor and his subcontractors.

like-kind property A tax term used in certain real property exchanges. Property must be exchanged for like kind property and the tax consequences postponed pursuant to Section 1031 of the Internal Revenue Code.

limited partnership A partnership created under state law which consists of one or more general partners who conduct the business and are responsible for any losses, and one or more special or limited partners who contribute capital and are liable only up to the amount contributed.

listing agreement An agreement between a real estate broker to assist in the sale or lease of that property in return for a fee, commission or other form of compensation. *See also* "Exclusive Listing Agreement."

long term lease A lease whose term exceeds ten years from initial signing until the date of expiration or renewal option.

lot A parcel of land, generally part of a series of parcels which make up a subdivision, the boundaries of which are created by and shown on a "plat."

low rise A building with fewer than seven stories above ground level.

lump-sum contract A construction contract requiring the contractor to complete a building for a specified amount, usually established by competitive bidding. The contractor absorbs any loss or retains any profit.

MAI Member of Appraisal Institute

maker One who executes (i.e., signs) a note in the capacity of the maker (i.e., borrower).

market indicators Statistical measures of construction and real estate activity, including issued permits, indices of building costs, deeds recorded and homes for sale.

market price The price a property brings in a given market. Commonly used interchangeably with market value, although not truly the same. *See also* "Market Value."

market rent The rental income that a property would most probably command on the open market, indicated by current rents paid and asked for comparable space as of the date of the appraisal. Market Rent: *See also* "Economic Rent."

market study A forecast of future demand for a type of project along with recommendations as the quantity to be sold or leased and prices to be charged. Also called Marketability Study.

marketable title Title to real property that can be readily marketed (i.e., sold) to a reasonably prudent purchaser aware of the facts and their legal meaning concerning liens and encumbrances.

market value The most probable price which a property should bring in a competitive and open market under all conditions requisite to a fair sale, the buyer and seller, each acting prudently and knowledgeably, and assuming the price is not affected by undue stimulus. Implicit in this definition is the consummation of a sale as of a specific date and passing of title from seller to buyer under conditions whereby: (1) buyer and seller are typically motivated; (2) both parties are well informed or well advised, and acting in what they consider their own best interests; (3) a reasonable time is allowed for exposure in the open market; (4) payment is made in terms of cash in U.S. dollars or in terms of financial arrangements comparable thereto; and (5) the price represents the normal consideration for the property sold unaffected by special or creative financial or sales concessions granted by anyone associated with the sale.

master lease A primary lease that controls subsequent leases and which may cover more property than subsequent leases.

master plan (1) A zoning plan for an entire governmental subdivision (e.g., a city). A comprehensive plan to allow a city to grow in an orderly manner, both economically and ecologically. (2) A developer's plan for a multi-phase office park or mixed-use development that takes into account all proposed or projected uses, improvements and amenities.

mechanic's lien A claim created by state statutes for the purpose of securing priority of payment for the price or value of work performed and materials furnished in construction or repair of improvements to land, and which attaches to the land as well as to the improvements.

metes and bounds The boundary lines of land described in accordance with their terminal points and angles. Originally metes referred to distance and bounds referred to direction. Today the words have no individual meaning of practical significance.

mid-rise A building with between seven and 25 stories above ground level.

mixed-use Space within a building or project provided for more than one use (e.g., an apartment building with office space, a hotel with office space, or a retail establishment with apartments).

mortgage The instrument that evidences an interest in real estate and created to provide a pledge as security for the performance or repayment of a loan. The borrower (i.e., mortgagor) retains possession and use of the property.

mortgagee The party that lends the money and receives the mortgage.

mortgagor The party that borrows the money and gives the mortgage on the property.

net absorption Absorption is a measure of the amount of office space leased over a period of the total square feet leased over a period of time taking into consideration office space vacated in the same area during the same period. *See also* "Gross Absorption."

net lease A lease in which the tenant pays, in addition to rent, certain costs associated with a leased property, including property taxes, insurance premiums, repairs, utilities, and maintenance. There are also "net-net" (double net) and "net-net-net" (triple net) leases, depending upon the degree to which the tenant is responsible for operating costs. *See also* "Gross Lease."

net rentable area Floor area of a building less any vertical penetrations of the floors. No deductions are made for necessary columns and projections of the building (BOMA Standard).

non-competitive space Space in office buildings which contain or are intended to contain one office occupant so that the space is rarely if ever available for lease or sublease.

non-recourse loan A loan that does not allow for a deficiency judgment against a borrower in the event of default. The borrower cannot be held personably liable. The lender's only available recourse in the event of default is the collateral or property.

nonjudicial foreclosure sale A property sale by a trustee under a deed of trust, or a mortgage under a power of sale of a mortgage.

open space The total area of land and/or water not improved by a building, structure, street, road or parking area, or containing only such improvements as are complementary, necessary or appropriate to the use and enjoyment of the open area.

operating expenses The actual cost of operating income-producing property, including utilities and similar day-to-day expenses, taxes, insurance, and reserves for the replacement of items that wear out.

operating cost escalation Refers to the clause in a lease agreement used to adjust rents over the term of a lease.

ownership Rights to the use, enjoyment, and alienation of property to the exclusion of others.

parking index Figure representing the number of parking spaces available per 1,000 square feet of gross leasable area.

partial taking The taking of part of an owner's property under the laws of eminent domain. Compensation must be based on damages or benefits to the remaining property as well as the portion taken.

pass throughs Building and operating expenses that are paid by the tenant under the terms of a lease.

PE Professional Engineer building and operating expenses that are paid by the tenant under the terms of a lease.

percentage lease A lease, generally on a retail business property, in which rent is calculated as a percentage of sales. There is usually a minimum or "base" rent in the event of poor sales.

performance bond A bond posted by a contractor guaranteeing the owner that the bonding company will complete construction if the contractor defaults.

"phantom" space Generally refers to space that is under lease to a tenant but not presently occupied. Usually created when a tenant consolidates or reduces operations in space it leases prior to the end of its lease term. The vacant but leased space may or may not be formally marketed on a sublet basis or counted among a market's vacancy.

PITI (principal, interest, taxes, and insurance) Acronym used to indicate what is included in a monthly mortgage payment on real property. Principal, interest, taxes and insurance are the four major portions of a typical monthly payment.

planned delivery space Office space that is currently under construction or renovation and will be completed (delivered to the market) within two years. Does not include Proposed or Future Proposed Space.

plat (plat map) A map dividing a parcel of land into lots, as in a subdivision.

power of sale Clause in a mortgage or deed of trust giving the mortgagee or trustee the power to sell the property in the event of default.

precast concrete Concrete building components fabricated at a plant site and shipped to the site of construction.

prelease A signed lease for space in a multi-tenant office building that has not yet received a Certificate of Occupancy.

prime space First generation (new) space that is currently available for lease but has never before been occupied by a tenant.

prime tenant The major tenant in a building, shopping center, etc.

proffer A development plan and/or written condition that, when offered by an owner and accepted by the county, becomes a legally binding part of the property in question.

punch list An itemized list noting incomplete or unsatisfactory construction. Usually prepared by the tenant architect after the contractor has notified the owner that the tenant space is substantially complete.

quitclaim deed A deed operating as a release and, as such, intended to pass to the grantee any title, interest, or claim that the grantor may have in the property, but not containing any warranty of valid interest or title in the grantor.

RA Resident Architect

raw land Land in its natural state. Land that has not been subdivided into lots, does not have water, sewers, streets, utilities, or other improvements necessary before a structure can be constructed.

REO (Real Estate Owned) All real estate directly owned by a lender, including real estate taken to satisfy a debt. Includes real estate acquired by lenders through foreclosure; or in settlement of any other obligations to the lender.

real property (1) Land and anything permanently affixed to the land, such as buildings, fences, and those things attached to the buildings, such as light fixtures, plumbing and heating fixtures, or other items which would be personal property if not attached. (2) May refer to rights in real property as well as the property itself.

recapture That portion of the gain from the sale of real estate that is taxed at ordinary income tax rates. Calculated as the difference between the accelerated depreciation taken and the straight-line depreciation that would have been allowed.

recourse The right of a lender or holder of a note secured by a mortgage to look to the personal assets of the borrower or endorser for payment should, not just to the property.

rehab A building undergoing extensive renovation in order to cure obsolescence. Some rehab projects are so extensive that tenants may not be in the building during the work period.

renewal option The right of a tenant to renew (i.e., extend the term of) a lease for a stated period of time and rent at an amount that can be determined.

rent Consideration paid for the occupancy and use of real property. A general term covering any consideration (not only money).

rent commencement date The date on which a tenant begins paying rent. Depending upon the nature of the marketplace, it may coincide with the lease commencement date or it may be several months after. It will never begin before the lease commencement date.

rentable square feet Usable square feet plus a percentage (the core factor) of the common areas on the floor, including hallways, bathrooms, and telephone closets. (And sometimes main lobbies.) Rentable square footage is the number of square feet on which a tenant's rent is based.

rentable/usable ratio The number resulting from dividing the Total Rentable Area in a building by the Usable Area. The inverse of this ratio describes the proportion of space that an occupant can expect to utilize.

rental concession See "Abatement."

rent-up period The period of time following construction of a new building when tenants are actively sought and the project is approaching stabilized occupancy.

right of first refusal See "First Refusal Right."

RPA Real Property Administrator

running with the land The term is generally synonymous with and usually used in reference to easements and covenants. It also means passing with the transfer of the land.

sale-leaseback A financing arrangement in which a property owner sells all or part of the property to an investor and then leases it back. Although the lease actually follows the sale, both are agreed to as part of the same transaction.

second mortgage A mortgage that ranks after a first mortgage in priority. Properties may have two, three, or more mortgages, deeds of trust, or land contracts as liens at the same time. Legal priority determines the designation first, second, etc.

secondary space Space that has been previously occupied and becomes available for lease. Includes both relet and sublet space.

security deposit Generally, a deposit of money by a tenant with a landlord to secure performance of a lease.

seisen (seizen) The term originally referred to the completion of feudal investiture by which a tenant was admitted into the field to render services to the lord or proprietor. Today it has come to mean possession under a legal right (usually a fee interest).

setback The distance from a lot line or other reference point, within which no structure may be located.

setback ordinance Part of a zoning ordinance that regulates the distance from the lot line to the point where improvements may be constructed.

site analysis The study of a specific parcel of land (and the surrounding area) to determine its suitability for a specific use.

site development All improvements made to a site before a building may be constructed, such as grading, utility installation, etc.

site plan A detailed plan, to scale, depicting development of a parcel of land and containing all information required by the zoning ordinance. *See also* "Master Plan."

slab The exposed wearing surface laid over the structural support beams of a building.

soft dollars That portion of equity investment that may be tax-deductible in the first year. *See also* "Hard Dollars."

space plan Sometimes called the preliminary plan. A graphic representation of a tenant's office space requirements, showing wall and door locations, room sizes, and some furniture layouts.

special assessment Any special charge levied against real property for public improvements (e.g., sidewalks, sewers, etc.) that benefit the assessed property.

specific performance A lawsuit in which the court compels one of the parties to perform or carry out the provisions of a contract into which he has entered.

speculative space Any prime space that has not been leased to a tenant prior to commencing construction on a new building.

step-up lease (graded lease) A lease calling for set increases in rent at set intervals.

straight lease (flat lease) A lease calling for the same amount of rent to be paid periodically (usually monthly) for the entire term of the lease.

strip center Any shopping area, generally with common parking, comprised of a row of stores.

subcontractor One who works under a general contractor; often a specialist, such as an electrical contractor, cement contractor, etc.

subdivision plat A detailed drawing, to scale, depicting division of a parcel of land into two or more lots and containing engineering considerations and other information required.

subordination agreement An agreement by which the priority of a mortgage lender is relinquished in favor of that of a lender who would otherwise be junior in status.

surety One who voluntarily binds himself to be obligated for the debt or obligation of another. A common example is the co-maker of a note. Surety differs from guarantor, although the terms are commonly (and mistakenly) used interchangeably.

surface rights The rights (i.e., easements) to use the surface of land, including the right to drill or mine through the surface when subsurface rights are involved.

survey The measurement of the boundaries of a parcel of land, its area and sometimes its topography.

taking A common synonym for condemnation or eminent domain.

tax base Assessed valuation of real property, which is multiplied by the tax rate to determine the amount of tax due.

tax lien (1) A lien for nonpayment of property taxes. Attaches only to the property upon which the taxes are unpaid. (2) A federal income tax lien. May attach to all property of the person owing the taxes.

tax roll A list containing the descriptions of all parcels in the country, the names of the owners (or those receiving the tax bill), assessed values and tax amounts.

tenant (1) A holder of property under a lease. (2) Originally, one who had the right to possession, irrespective of the title interest.

tenant at will One who holds possession of premises by permission of the owner or landlord, but without agreement for a fixed term.

tenant improvements Improvements to land or buildings to meet the needs of tenants. May be new improvements or remodeling, and may be paid for by the landlord, the tenant, or shared. *See also* "Leasehold Improvements," "Workletter."

"time is of the essence" Clause used in contracts to bind one party to performance at or by a specified time in order to bind the other party to performance.

title The means whereby one has just and full possession of real property.

title insurance Insurance against loss resulting from defects of title to a specifically described parcel of real property. Defects may run to the fee (i.e., chain of title) or to encumbrances.

title search A review of all recorded documents affecting a specific piece of property to determine the present condition of title.

total inventory Total square footage of rentable office or industrial space, vacant and occupied, ready for tenant finish. Includes owner-occupied space.

trade fixtures Personal property used in a business and attached to a structure, but removable upon sale because it is deemed to be part of the business, not of the real estate.

triple net (NNN) rent Rent stipulated in a lease in which a tenant agrees to pay a share of the landlord's operating expenses or real estate taxes for the building proportionate to the amount of space it occupies. *See also* "Full Service Rent."

turnkey project A project in which the developer is responsible for the total completion of a building (including interior design and construction) or demised premises to the customized requirements of a future owner or tenant.

under construction Planned buildings for which construction has started but have not yet been granted a Certificate of Occupancy. Planned buildings are not included.

under contract A property, for which a purchase offer has been accepted by the seller, is said to be "under contract." Generally, the prospective buyer is given a certain period of time in which to perform feasibility studies and finalize financing arrangements. During the time, the seller cannot entertain offers from other buyers unless the purchase contract is allowed to expire without going to closing.

unencumbered Describes title to property that is free of liens and any other encumbrances. Free and clear.

unimproved land Most commonly refers to land without buildings; it can also mean land in its natural state. *See also* "Raw Land."

use Specific purpose, for which a parcel of land or a building is designed, arranged, intended, occupied, or maintained.

vacancy factor The amount of gross revenue lost because of vacant space; an allowance item on pro formap income statements, usually calculated as a percentage of gross revenue.

vacancy rate A measurement expressed as a percentage of the total amount of available space compared to the total inventory of space. Computed by multiplying vacant space times 100 and divided by total inventory.

vacant space Existing space, which is currently being marketed for sale or lease, excluding sublet space.

variance A permit that grants a property owner relief from certain provisions of a zoning ordinance when, because of the particular physical surroundings, shape or topographical condition of the property, compliance would result in a particular hardship or practical difficulty which would deprive the owner of the reasonable use of the land or building involved.

vendee Purchaser or "buyer," generally used in real property context.

vendor The person who transfers property by sale. Another word for "seller." Commonly used in land contract sales.

warranty A binding promise made at the time of sale whereby the seller gives the buyer certain assurances as to the condition of the property.

wear and tear The deterioration or loss in value caused by the tenant's normal and reasonable use. In many leases the tenant is not responsible for "normal wear and tear."

weighted average rental rates Rental rates averaged to the amount of space available in each building per market area.

workletter The standard building items that the landlord contributes as part of the tenant improvements. Examples of standard building items are doors, partitions, lights, floor covering, telephone outlets, etc. The Workletter by specify the quantity and quality of the materials to be used and often carries a dollar value.

working drawings The set of plans for a project that, in combination with a set of specifications comprise the contract documents indicating the exact manner in which a project should be built. *See also* "Contract Documents."

workout The process by which a borrower attempts to negotiate with a lender to restructure the borrower's debt rather than go through fore-closure proceedings.

zoning A method of regulating use of real estate by dividing a city or other area into zones and des-ignating which uses may be permitted for land in each zone.

zoning ordinance The set of laws and regulations, generally at the city or county level, that control the use of land and construction of improve-ments in a given area or zone.

liens against license (liquor)
environmentals — gas station — cleaned and cleared by one engineer
bank wanted second firm to do environmental

SBA loans   25 years
       10% down

beware of balloons or rate review clauses in finance agreements w/banks

depreciate building — not land ⟹ outline
Handicap accessibility — doorways / bathrooms /
Certificate of good standing
              State taxes
              property taxes
              supplies

Zoning — Floor Area (Covered) Ratio

Unofficial Guide to Real Estate Investing
       Martin & Strauss

Small Business Development Center

up your cash flow (software

Cherrystone Group

everycompanycounts.com